CONTENTS

BARRON'S BOOK NOTES

ERNEST HEMINGWAY'S

The Sun Also Rises

BY

Robert Dunn

SERIES EDITOR

Michael Spring
Editor, *Literary Cavalcade*
Scholastic Inc.

BARRON'S

BARRON'S EDUCATIONAL SERIES, INC.
Woodbury, New York / London / Toronto / Sydney

ACKNOWLEDGMENTS

We would like to acknowledge the many painstaking hours of work Holly Hughes and Thomas F. Hirsch have devoted to making the *Book Notes* series a success.

All inquiries should be addressed to:
Barron's Educational Series, Inc.
113 Crossways Park Drive
Woodbury, New York 11797

Library of Congress Catalog Card No. 84-18494

International Standard Book No. 0-8120-3443-0

Library of Congress Cataloging in Publication Data
Dunn, Robert, 1950–
    Ernest Hemingway's the sun also rises.

    (Barron's book notes)
    Bibliography: p. 82
    Summary: A guide to reading "The Sun Also Rises"
with a critical and appreciative mind. Includes
background on the author's life and times, sample tests,
term paper suggestions, and a reading list.
    1. Hemingway, Ernest, 1899–1961. Sun also rises.
[1. Hemingway, Ernest, 1899–1961. Sun also rises.
2. American literature—History and criticism]
I. Title. II. Series.
PS3515.E37S923 1984   813'.52   84-18494
ISBN 0-8120-3443-0 (pbk.)

PRINTED IN THE UNITED STATES OF AMERICA

456   550   987654321

ADVISORY BOARD

HOW TO USE THIS BOOK

You have to know how to approach literature in order to get the most out of it. This *Barron's Book Notes* volume follows a plan based on methods used by some of the best students to read a work of literature.

Begin with the guide's section on the author's life and times. As you read, try to form a clear picture of the author's personality, circumstances, and motives for writing the work. This background usually will make it easier for you to hear the author's tone of voice, and follow where the author is heading.

Then go over the rest of the introductory material—such sections as those on the plot, characters, setting, themes, and style of the work. Underline, or write down in your notebook, particular things to watch for, such as contrasts between characters and repeated literary devices. At this point, you may want to develop a system of symbols to use in marking your text as you read. (Of course, you should only mark up a book you own, not one that belongs to another person or a school.) Perhaps you will want to use a different letter for each character's name, a different number for each major theme of the book, a different color for each important symbol or literary device. Be prepared to mark up the pages of your book as you read. Put your marks in the margins so you can find them again easily.

Now comes the moment you've been waiting for—the time to start reading the work of literature. You may want to put aside your *Barron's Book Notes* volume until you've read the work all the way through. Or you may want to alternate, reading the *Book Notes* analysis of each section as soon as you have finished reading the corresponding part of the original. Before you move on, reread crucial passages you don't fully understand. (Don't take this guide's analysis for granted—make up your own mind as to what the work means.)

Once you've finished the whole work of literature, you may want to review it right away, so you can firm up your ideas about what it means. You may want to leaf through the book concentrating on passages you marked in reference to one character or one theme. This is also a good time to reread the *Book Notes* introductory material, which pulls together insights on specific topics.

When it comes time to prepare for a test or to write a paper, you'll already have formed ideas about the work. You'll be able to go back through it, refreshing your memory as to the author's exact words and perspective, so that you can support your opinions with evidence drawn straight from the work. Patterns will emerge, and ideas will fall into place; your essay question or term paper will almost write itself. Give yourself a dry run with one of the sample tests in the guide. These tests present both multiple-choice and essay questions. An accompanying section gives answers to the multiple-choice questions as well as suggestions for writing the essays. If you have to select a term paper topic, you may choose one from the list of suggestions in this book. This guide also provides you with a reading list, to help you when you start research for a term paper, and a selection of provocative comments by critics, to spark your thinking before you write.

THE AUTHOR
AND HIS TIMES

Before World War I, which was fought from 1914 to 1918, America was hopeful and optimistic. There was a spirit of reform in the land—man could be perfected, many believed—and after a century of world peace a great war was beyond all memory or imagination. Then the world war dropped like a sudden storm out of a clear sky, and by the time it was over the whole world had changed. Europe, the battlefield, was devastated. More than that, though, the social order was irredeemably shattered. Nations had plunged into modern, mechanized warfare, and the carnage was immense. The unimaginable horror of that experience has haunted us ever since.

Those who came of age then were faced with finding a way to live in an unrecognizable world. One of the first books to explore the values and life-styles of this so-called Lost Generation of American youth was *The Sun Also Rises*. Although it takes place in 1924, nearly seven years after World War I ended, all the characters are still burdened by their war experience.

Many young Americans went to Europe, especially Paris, in the years right after the armistice. The attractions were several. Many of these Americans had served and so were the first members of their immediate families ever to see Europe. They found it exotic compared to life at home, so after the war they returned. They also felt at home in a culture of displaced people, many of whom had settled in Paris. Things not allowed back home—smoking, drinking, casual sex, and other exuberant traits of youth—were the norm in certain parts of the city. They liked to stay up all night talking and drinking in cafés, and then watch dawn break over the River Seine. Their nights were a whirl of talk about writers, art (Picasso, Matisse, and other founders of modern art were in Paris then), and style. Also—no small matter—there was a terrifically favorable exchange rate: a few dollars from home could go a long way in postwar Paris.

The Sun Also Rises is set among these expatriates who purposefully left their native land. Hemingway didn't have to look far to find models for the characters in his novel, for he himself was an expatriate, and *The Sun Also Rises* is closely based on an actual trip Hemingway and his friends took from Paris to Spain a month before he began the book. What makes the book a work of art is that it is not simply a record of something that happened, it's a fully imagined rendering of his own experience. *The Sun Also Rises* was a sensation when it was published; numerous young people recognized themselves in the book, even if they had never been to Paris or seen a bullfight.

Hemingway wrote about heroes because he saw himself as a hero, too. His public saw him as one also, and newspapers followed his later exploits as they did the lives of movie stars.

Hemingway was born in 1899 in Oak Park, a suburb of Chicago. In high school he was an all-American boy, a good student and a successful athlete. Hemingway never went to college, however, and all his life he held a public disdain for academic life, preferring a life of action. When he graduated from high school he became a cub reporter on the *Kansas City Star*. World War I started, and he went to Italy as a volunteer Red

Cross ambulance driver. He was at the front for only a week when he was hit by fragments of a mortar shell and then cut down by machine-gun fire as he helped carry a more severely wounded man to safety. He spent three months in a hospital in Milan, undergoing a dozen operations. Many observers believe it was during this hospital stay that he acquired his hard-nosed vision of life. He must have gone over the moments of his near-death again and again, believing that if he could understand his sensations at every moment, he could understand what happened to him and move beyond it. Serious wounds received in other wars and on expeditions in Africa left him emotionally scarred for life, but he was always able to transform these experiences into art.

Jake Barnes, the hero of *The Sun Also Rises*, also has a war wound; for him, it's a badge that certifies he knows the truth about life. Like Hemingway, perhaps, Jake never recovers emotionally from his wound. He needs (as Hemingway did) a light to sleep by in order to get through the night.

After the war Hemingway returned to Michigan, grew disenchanted with America, married Hadley, the first of four wives, and returned to Paris. He worked as a reporter for a Toronto paper, and due to the high cost of telegraphing copy, worked at getting as much information into as few words as possible. He also wrote short stories set mostly in Michigan, and precisely worded prose pieces about his war experiences in the Crimea, which were published in his first book, *In Our Time*.

Hemingway soon became the most famous American expatriate in Paris. What made him different from most of the café loungers who wanted to be writers

was that he had more talent and he worked harder—
struggling day after day to perfect his style.

The Sun Also Rises was written in less than a year,
and after massive cutting (including the first few
chapters excised by Hemingway's friend, F. Scott Fitzgerald), was published in 1926. Only 27, Hemingway
was instantly recognized as a new and important literary voice. Three years later his second novel, *A Farewell to Arms*, made him even more famous.

For the rest of his life Hemingway's books and his
life were intertwined. Later novels ran from well-
received (*For Whom the Bell Tolls*) to very poorly
received (*Across the River and Into the Trees*), but none
strayed far from the study of a hero adrift in the modern world and the personal code that gives him guid-
ance. Dashing from one exotic place to another; cov-
ering the Spanish Civil War as a reporter; hobnobbing
with World War II soldiers; playing Daddy to the
famous actress Marlene Dietrich—this was Hemingway, an irresistible figure for the popular press. He
always took his writing seriously, but as time went on
it became clear, both to his critics and to himself, that
his best work was behind him. To many who knew
him he became in his later years a parody of his heroic
self. In 1961, beset with severe aches from all his inju-
ries, and deeply depressed, he shot himself in Ketch-
um, Idaho, and died immediately.

Hemingway's legacy to us, besides some fine
books, is his style and his sense of the hero. When he
began writing, his lean, emphatic style was a great
change from the florid, sentimental prose of almost all
his contemporaries. In Paris he was a friend of the
poet Ezra Pound, who was working to achieve sharp,
true images, and of Gertrude Stein, who believed in
using only the simplest words in interesting rhythms
and repetitions. Hemingway learned their lessons

well. He described his own style as putting "down what I see and what I feel in the best and simplest way I can tell it." At his purest, he forsook metaphor and even adjectives as unnecessary adornments; he wrote mainly with simple nouns and verbs, simple words that made clean, swift motions. Hemingway also believed in concealing more than he showed. Good writing should be like an iceberg, he said; a writer should only show one-eighth of what he knows. In *The Sun Also Rises* you'll find much that is hidden. Relationships between characters are revealed by a nod of the head, or even by the absence of an expected nod. The book has to be read carefully, with your imagination supplying the "seven-eighths of information" that Hemingway left out.

In recent years much scorn has been heaped on the Hemingway hero. We think we know the type: a macho male always bragging about how big and strong he is. Everything he does is a test of manliness; if he doesn't take chances, even foolish ones, he's a coward or effeminate; if he hurts, he doesn't cry but holds everything in. To us there's something funny and old-fashioned in such a caricature of a man. But like most popular images this picture of a Hemingway hero is only a partial portrait. The truth is more complex.

Certainly Hemingway hated anything effeminate in a man, but there's much evidence to suggest that his macho image was a mask that covered his insecurities about his own manhood. As be became more famous he modeled his own image on the tragic heroes of his books, but he was never quite convincing. Many observers now believe he acted as he did—loud, braggartly, domineering—because inside him his talent was drying up. They see Hemingway as a tragic figure, a victim of his own self-hype.

In *The Sun Also Rises* the question of who is a hero is central. You will find that Jake Barnes, the narrator, has the outline of a hero, but that he is basically weak, impotent, and a party to the corruption of the true hero, Pedro Romero. When Hemingway creates fabled heroes like Jake Barnes, he shows them in an unsparing light: riddled with anxieties, ultimately unsure of themselves and their manhood, and unable to hold to their code of manly behavior. Hemingway's heroes are not made of cardboard but of flesh and blood; they don't soar away at the end, like Superman, but crash in failure.

Hemingway, too, finally crashed in failure. Many believe that ultimately two contemporaries, William Faulkner and F. Scott Fitzgerald, were of greater literary stature. But in his day Hemingway was the most influential. Even now when you see a man wearing a shirt unbuttoned to his waist to show off a hairy chest, you're seeing a version of the Hemingway hero. When people talk about ''The Right Stuff'' or ''What It Takes to Be a Man,'' they're usually discussing behavior in Hemingway's terms. The great advantage of reading *The Sun Also Rises* closely is that Hemingway shows us the truth behind the caricature; he lets us see his own ambiguities, honest failings, and sincerely tragic vision of life.

THE NOVEL

The Plot

A group of young Americans is living in Paris in the years after World War I. Before the war they might have become bankers or lawyers, but the experience of so much death and destruction undermined their belief in traditional American values, and sent them off to Paris in search of new experiences. Now they're living as artists and writers, going from café to café, drinking too much, gossiping more than working, and exploring a new sexual freedom.

Robert Cohn, a Jew who went to Princeton (where he found himself an outsider in a predominately White Anglo-Saxon Protestant culture), and Jake Barnes, a newspaperman, are two of these American expatriates. Jake is in love with a beautiful but mannish British woman, Lady Brett Ashley, but their love can't be consummated because Jake has a wound around his genitals and cannot make love. Cohn, like most other men, falls madly in love with Lady Brett the moment he meets her. He's an old-fashioned romantic, believing in true love and chivalry—in sharp contrast to Brett, Jake, and all their jaded, hard-boiled friends, who believe that nothing, especially love, has much of a chance to survive in this fallen, postwar world. Only superficial pleasures are left for these "survivors," and sex is one of their favorites. Since Jake can't satisfy her, Brett goes off for a tryst in Spain with Robert Cohn.

Meanwhile, Brett's fiancé Michael Campbell and a writer named Bill Gorton arrive in Paris. Jake has planned a trip to Pamplona, Spain, for the famous festival of San Fermín, which is highlighted by the running of bulls through the streets, and a week of bullfights. The whole gang—Jake, Brett, Mike, Bill, even Robert Cohn—decide to go. This creates some complicated relationships, since Brett, like a queen, is surrounded by three suitors, all of whom feel they deserve her affection. Brett is a free spirit, though, and loses interest in her men; in fact, no sooner does she get to Pamplona than she sets her sights on another man, the bullfighter Pedro Romero.

Before the festivities Jake and Bill go fishing up into the Spanish Pyrenees, where they restore themselves in nature. The countryside soothes while the civilized city chafes. But their idyll ends, and they head back to Pamplona.

Brett, Mike, and Robert Cohn are already there. Mike and Brett had taken their own side trip to San Sebastian, and Cohn had joined them. He wasn't wanted, but he felt he owned Brett, and made a nuisance of himself all weekend. Now in Pamplona, he continues to follow Brett around like a lovesick puppy.

Jake is no less lovesick, but he holds his feelings in, except when he's alone at night. Then he's not so tough. He is tortured by the sounds of Brett and Mike laughing in a nearby room. He curses the wound that makes him less than a man, and curses Brett for tempting him. He even curses the Catholic Church, in which he once believed, because it can no longer help him. Finally, in tears, and with a nightlight burning, he falls asleep.

The festival begins. Dancers appear, carrying Brett as if she were their goddess. Jake and Bill meet Pedro Romero, a handsome, 19-year-old bullfighter who best exemplifies what readers call the Hemingway hero. Romero is a professional, passionately devoted to his art. He does his job cleanly and concisely, without grandstand flourishes. Brett falls for him, and Jake, still in despair, arranges for the two of them to get together.

When Robert Cohn hears what Jake has done, he calls Jake a pimp. Jake swings at him, but Cohn was a college boxer and knocks Jake out. Throughout the trip Mike has been taunting and insulting Cohn, and now Cohn knocks Mike down, too. On a rampage, Cohn finds Brett and Romero together and beats Romero black and blue. Romero is outclassed in size and boxing skill, but he fights tenaciously. Afterward a guilt-ridden Cohn apologizes to Jake, and then leaves Pamplona.

The bulls are run through the streets, and a Spanish peasant is lifted on a bull's horns and gored to death. The whole town turns out for his funeral. On the last day of the bullfights, Romero shines. He fights a difficult bull with calm grace, then finishes off the bull that gored the peasant and is awarded the bull's ear. He gives the bloody ear to Brett as a love token.

The festival over, everybody leaves—Brett to Madrid with Romero; Mike to a French border town where he has credit at a bar; Bill back to Paris. Jake goes to San Sebastian to relax for a while. He reads, swims, eats well, talks to the townspeople—and then receives a telegram from Brett: she needs help in Madrid.

When Jake arrives he finds that Romero wanted to marry Brett. Because of his youth and innocence, however, she was afraid of corrupting him, and turned him down. She's pleased at her act—it was so wonderfully moral—but she also feels lonely. She's glad Jake has come, she has really loved only him. But their love is impossible, and when she wistfully thinks how happy they might have been, Jake, with bittersweet irony, replies, "Isn't it pretty to think so?" Nothing, we learn, will improve for these people. If they're lost, they won't be found; if they're forsaken, they won't be redeemed.

The Characters

Jake Barnes

Jake is an American in his mid-20s working as a journalist in Paris after World War I. His disillusionment and unsentimental view of reality are shared by many young Americans who left America to live in Europe. Jake's life in Paris consists of going from café to café, drinking, eating too much, talking the night away, and watching the sexual antics of his friends.

The most important thing about Jake is the wound around his groin, which he received on the Italian front during the war. Though it's not clear exactly what the wound is, it keeps him from having sexual relations, though he can still feel desire.

The woman he loves is Lady Brett Ashley, and she loves him, but they can't stay together because of his wound. They tried once, but their inability to consummate their love left them both terribly frustrated. Unable to keep the woman he loves, Jake finds himself standing on the sidelines, watching her have affairs with his friends. On one occasion he actually fixes her up with another man, a bullfighter named Pedro Romero.

Jake's given name is Jacob, after the Biblical character who wrestles all night with the angel. Jake wrestles, too, with himself and with his demons, and also with the postwar modern world. Finally he reaches an unsatisfactory peace with his life.

Jake tells us the story of *The Sun Also Rises* in the first person. It's important to keep in mind that not everything he tells us is necessarily the truth. What we learn from him is colored by his attitudes, his experience, and his wound.

Jake is judgmental. One of his goals is to figure out how to live in the modern world; that is, how to act and how to determine the difference between right and wrong in a world seemingly without meaning or direction. As readers we should always ask whether his judgments are the same as our own.

Although Hemingway never made the comparison, many critics compare Jake to a mythological figure called the Fisher King, whose well-being mirrored the well-being of his nation. The Fisher King, like Jake, was impotent, and as a result his land became sterile and incapable of growing food. In the myth the Fisher King is healed, and his land turns bountiful. But Jake is not healed in *The Sun Also Rises*, and neither is his world.

Jake is an archetypal tough guy hero, a man who doesn't show his feelings. He loves to hunt and fish. He's proud. Though he's a cynical, clearsighted realist, he's soft at the center. When he's alone at night we see him start to fall apart from the strain of being impotent. He can't sleep without a nightlight because he's afraid of the dark.

Jake, like his friends, is empty inside. While others might have religion to fill the void, Jake, though he says he's a Catholic, doesn't really believe in religion any longer. He believes that he should believe, but he can't.

Yet Jake also is a hero. More than his friends, he tries to understand what is good and of lasting value. He wishes he was able to live by these values. He has passion, courage, a blistering honesty, and, no small matter, a gift for friendship. What he doesn't have is love, faith, and purpose. But there is little love, faith, and purpose in the wasteland world of *The Sun Also*

Rises; and so, finally, it's not Jake's failure we must condemn or pity, but the greater failure of the world he lives in.

Lady Brett Ashley

Lady Brett is a 34-year-old Englishwoman who is beautiful and emotionally scarred. She had an innocent love affair when she was a volunteer nurse in the war, but ever since her young soldier died, she has drifted from one worthless man to another. Her husband, a British Lord from whom she is separated, gave her her title, but also made her sleep on the floor and more than once threatened her with a gun.

Now she runs around Paris with a group of homosexuals. She is engaged to Michael Campbell, a drunk and bankrupt Scot, but she has numerous affairs. She also loves Jake Barnes, but because of his wound, they can't make love; their relationship only frustrates them both. Like Jake, she is a hardboiled realist.

Lady Brett represents everything that offends the prevalent sensibilities of her time. She smokes and drinks too much. She is in the process of a divorce, and is promiscuous. She has no religion and no strong moral beliefs. In short, she is irresponsible and neurotic.

Brett is considered a goddess by the dancers at the Spanish fiesta. She is said to collect men, and indeed at one point all the principal men in the book—Jake, Robert Cohn, Mike, Bill, and Pedro Romero—are in love with her. One character calls her Circe, after the mythical woman who turns men to swine, and many readers see Brett as having an evil magic that emasculates men.

Brett herself is mannish and tries to act like the men she associates with. She has very short hair and often refers to herself as "one of the chaps." Sexual roles are

confused in *The Sun Also Rises*—the hero is impotent
and the heroine behaves like a man. This confusion
represents the perversion and failure of love Hemingway saw in the postwar world.

Brett is an example of an individual trying to cope in
a world that has lost the unquestioned moral order of
organized religion.

Robert Cohn

Robert Cohn is the most difficult character to understand. Jake, who describes him to us, comes to hate
him, and for good reason, since Cohn steals the woman Jake loves. Bill Gorton and Mike Campbell slander
Cohn at every turn with vicious anti-Semitic insults.
Jake and his friends all subscribe to a hardboiled code
of realism and can't tolerate a simple romantic like
Cohn. But don't let the other characters sway you in
your opinion of Cohn; you have to stand apart from
their prejudices and make up your own mind.

Robert Cohn is an outsider, as he has been all his
life. He was a Jew at Princeton at a time when almost
no Jews attended Ivy League schools. His family is
very rich, and he's had a privileged life that others
might envy. He's been able to have and to do whatever he wants. He has flirted with the arts, started a
small magazine, written a bad novel, and now lives
among other American writers in Paris.

Robert Cohn often doesn't know when and where
he belongs. He pursues Brett after she has made it
clear she doesn't want him. He has little self-knowl-
edge and cannot understand why his more worldly
wise friends make fun of him. But is he really so different? Apart from being Jewish and relatively inexpe-
rienced, Cohn is an expatriate much like his so-called
friends. The "in crowd" keeps him at a distance, how-

ever, because he's an effective scapegoat for their own failings.

Cohn's innocent romanticism sharply separates him from the others. He doesn't understand that the war has destroyed innocence, love, and trust. He believes that sleeping with Lady Brett on their trip to San Sebastian means they will love each other forever. For Brett, a collector of men, their romance means very little, but it takes a vicious insult and three fist-fights before Cohn understands how little Brett cares.

Jake and his friends have learned about life from life; Cohn has learned what he knows from books. He accepts illusions over realities, and this gets him into trouble. Yet, because he doesn't see the world as completely tarnished, he is not defeated by it. For Cohn, the world is a place of life and hope. He does not see it as a wasteland.

Cohn may remind you of a puppy in his need for love and acceptance. He slavers after the first woman who accepts him and lets her dominate him. He likes to be mothered. There is something pathetic about Cohn, maybe even tragic. He wants so much to belong—simply to be loved and cared for—and yet we know he'll never be accepted.

Yet Cohn also has strengths. At Princeton he was a champion boxer, and when he's finally forced to fight, he does so furiously. He knocks down Jake and Mike, and he attacks Romero, too. This fighting is noble in that it means Cohn will stand up for what he believes in, yet it is also stupid because it gets him nowhere. Cohn doesn't simply fight and walk away; he fights and then feels pathetically guilty about it. His last act is to beg forgiveness from Jake. Jake forgives him, though he knows he shouldn't. Jake also knows as well as we do that Cohn should never have asked to be forgiven.

In some ways Cohn is not that different from Jake. Both are grownup adolescents and both love Lady Brett hopelessly. As much as Jake tries to separate himself from Cohn—there is even a point at which we wonder why they're friends at all—we finally have to believe that they are simply two sides of the same coin. Cohn is a failed comic hero, Jake a failed tragic one.

Mike Campbell

Mike is a Scot who is engaged to Lady Brett Ashley. She has agreed to marry him after her divorce from Lord Ashley, but she later changes her mind.

Almost every time we see Mike he is pathetically drunk. He says vicious, stupid things about Robert Cohn and obnoxious things about Brett. Once wealthy, but now bankrupt, he runs up credit he knows he can't repay. By the end of the novel he is forced to borrow money to pay his hotel expenses.

Mike is a virulent anti-Semite who lashes out at Cohn whenever he is feeling frustrated and inadequate. We can criticize Mike for making Cohn a scapegoat; yet, because Cohn is trying to steal Brett, Mike has some reason to attack him.

Mike would like others to think he is strong, courageous, manly, and successful. He fails at this and drinks to forget his failure. Why, you'll want to ask, do his friends put up with him? Very likely they see a lot of Mike Campbell in themselves. To condemn him would be to condemn themselves, so they look instead at his positive side. Jake, for instance, points out that when Mike is sober he is very charming. From the evidence in the book, however, Mike is never sober and never charming.

Mike, Jake, Bill, and Brett belong to a clique that excludes Robert Cohn and others. Mike is not a very important character except to represent the worst characteristics of this group.

Bill Gorton

Bill Gorton is a successful American writer and an old friend of Jake's. He comes to Paris especially to go with the group to the fiesta in Spain. Bill also drinks too much and has a hard, cynical wit that is sometimes funny and sometimes simply cruel. In contrast to his friend Jake, who is trying hard to find something to believe in (and failing) Bill never seems to believe in anything at all. Another product—some would say casualty—of the war, he deals with life by mocking it.

It is Bill who joins Jake on the fishing idyll to the Irati River in Spain. He is loyal to Jake and other members of their clique, but to those he doesn't know or doesn't think he should accept, he's unkind and arrogant.

Of all these lost characters, Bill is one of the most lost, though he'd never admit it.

Pedro Romero

If any of the major characters remains untarnished by the modern world, it is the young, handsome bullfighter, Pedro Romero. Though he is only 19, he has made his name as a bullfighter and triumphantly kills the last bull at the fiesta.

Pedro Romero is a professional. He separates his work from himself, and he performs his work perfectly. He knows his art too well to care about showing off or using tricks. He gets very close to the bull and does his job "smoothly, calmly, and beautifully."

Romero is also an innocent. This is not only because he is young, but because he has something to believe in and to dedicate his life to: bullfighting. Bullfighting repays his dedication. None of the other characters believes in anything with the passion Romero gives to bullfighting.

Romero also believes in love. Much like Robert Cohn, he falls completely in love with Lady Brett. The difference between the two men, however, is that Romero never loses his dignity. He is always proud and determined. He does things to please himself, not others, and he always follows a strict code of behavior. He is fearless and intrepid—an unflawed hero.

All the other characters respect Romero. Brett respects him so much that even though she wants to stay with him, she leaves because she's afraid she'll corrupt him. One of the book's unanswered questions is whether Romero's purity could ever withstand Brett and the corruption of the modern world she represents. You'll have to decide for yourself whether you think Romero would, in a few years, become tarnished, too.

In terms of *The Sun Also Rises*, however, Romero is as close as any character comes to a hero. In comparison, all the other characters, especially Jake, are failures. Romero is important because he stands outside the modern wasteland. He represents tradition, ritual, passion, and faith. Bullfighting is a closed world of its own, and that's what keeps him pure. The other characters can only visit this world for a short time, as tourists going to the fiesta.

But remember, Romero is a young man. We don't see enough of him to know if or when he'll be corrupted, but we do see enough to know that he cannot cure people lost in the modern world.

Count Mippipopolous

The count is a rich, titled friend of Lady Brett who always gets good value for what he pays for, be it champagne or antiques. He has no use for God or anything that does not fit into his narrow scale of values. Whether he is capable of love is something you'll have to decide for yourself.

The count is plump and roly-poly, a fine comic creation. Ultimately, though, he's pathetic. He might be happier than Bill and Mike, for at least he has pleasure, but it's the easy pleasure that comes from instant material gratification. We have to wonder if he embraces any of the uncertainty in life that leads to surprise and grandeur. Maybe he has come to terms with the world too well; maybe, as Brett says, he is dead.

The count does have experience. He has seen much of the world. Like Jake, he has a wound—an arrow pierced his stomach. He is older than the other characters and perhaps the toughest. He is an image of what Jake and Brett could easily become.

Montoya

Montoya runs the hotel in Pamplona where Jake and his friends stay. He is perceptive enough to know who has real *afición* (passion) for bullfighting, and he will always find a room for those who share his passion, no matter how crowded his place is. He knows Romero has *afición*, and decides that Jake does, too. In a way, Montoya is the book's best judge of values. He finally decides that Jake's friends—Brett, Cohn, Mike, and Bill—are unworthy. He makes Jake feel ashamed of his friends, of the way he himself has behaved. When Jake leaves, Montoya won't even say good-bye to him.

Other Elements

SETTING

The Sun Also Rises is set in Europe after World War I. Except for the bullfighter Pedro Romero, all the major characters are expatriates from America and Great Britain. In search of adventure, and of something to fill the void in their lives, they have come to live in Paris.

Paris in the 1920s was famous for its thriving Bohemian café culture. Painters such as Picasso, Miró, and Matisse were there, as was an indomitable American woman named Gertrude Stein, who had established a famous salon where painters and writers such as James Joyce, F. Scott Fitzgerald, and Ernest Hemingway met and exchanged ideas.

The cultural movement known as Modernism was then coming into its own. Modernism reflected the cultural dislocation, the break with tradition, and the freedom to experiment of the postwar era. Much original art and writing was created during this time, including *The Sun Also Rises*. Hemingway's novel thus both captures and is an expression of the age in which it was written.

Hemingway's characters find life in Paris exciting, but also empty. To escape the sophistication and corruption of the city, they travel to the more traditional world of Spain.

The book's main characters—Jake, Brett, Robert Cohn, Mike, and Bill—are not tied to any one set of values and can skim from place to place like water skiers over a lake. In contrast, the natives of Paris and Pamplona seem to lead deeply rooted and stable lives. The expatriates move from one European setting to another, permanent tourists forever looking in at a world to which they do not belong.

THEMES

Love

Is there any evidence of joyful, fulfilling love in *The Sun Also Rises?* Hardly a trace. The two main characters, Jake and Brett, can't love either physically or emotionally. When they speak of the possibility of love, they are imagining life in another, better world. In the actual world they inhabit, both are wounded, Jake physically, Brett psychically. Neither is able to find any satisfaction or completeness in love.

Robert Cohn loves, but it's a silly, naïve love predicated on storybook romances. Cohn is immediately attracted to Brett. Because she's part curious, part bored, she goes off with him. What does their romance mean? For Brett, nothing; for Cohn, everything. He continues to believe against all evidence that theirs is a perfect love. He's wrong, of course, and all the other characters despise him for his blindness.

Mike, Brett's fiancé, is too drunk and insecure to love. Bill Gorton picks up an American girl at the fiesta, but nothing comes of it—he's too cynical to love.

That leaves Pedro Romero, the hero of Hemingway's code—a man young, innocent, passionate, and brave enough to love. He falls for Brett and wants to marry her. But Brett, knowing she'll ruin him, gives him up.

Religion

Does formal religion play a role in the lives of any of the characters? Does it satisfy anyone's need for faith? For these members of the Lost Generation, no. Brett feels uncomfortable in a church, Jake has turned away from Roman Catholicism (the church offered no consolation for his wound), and Robert Cohn, a Jew, seems indifferent to his faith.

The Wasteland

Many readers see a correspondence between *The Sun Also Rises* and T. S. Eliot's noted poem, "The Waste Land." The poem was published four years before the novel, and although Hemingway denied it, it seems to have influenced the book. The central figure in the poem is acknowledged by Eliot to be the Fisher King, as described in Jessie L. Weston's study of the Grail legend, *From Ritual to Romance.* The Fisher King had a sickness that kept him from reproducing. Because his personal health was reflected in the health of his country, his land remained sterile. Many readers see Jake Barnes as this impotent hero presiding over an infertile land. Though life in Paris is liberating for this young American, it is also decadent and essentially pointless. Only in the Spanish countryside does fertility abound. While fishing, Jake becomes well, but when he returns to his civilized friends he loses his health again.

The wasteland is a dead land, and those in it are dead-in-life. In the novel this death-in-life is found in an emotional sterility that infects all the characters. Only Brett regains some health when she gives up Romero. The greater rejuvenation that might be possible from a life with Jake is, for both of them, only a wistful dream.

Values

The Sun Also Rises is a portrait of Americans searching for new values in a world in which old standards have been blown away by war. Jake, the primary searcher, is interested in Count Mippipopolous, who seems to know exactly what he wants and how to get it. But the count's value system is simply to pay as little as possible for as much as possible—marvelous advice in a department store, but a little thin when applied to life.

Pedro Romero has a strong sense of right and wrong, but he doesn't talk about it. He simply does his job perfectly. He fights bulls and conducts his life with *afición*, or passion, which both Hemingway and his characters greatly admire. Romero's *afición* is as untarnished and pure as the bullfighter himself. Is this because he comes from a land that was relatively untouched by the war?

Most of the characters have settled for empty rounds of drinking and sex in Paris. Romero is different. He doesn't need to buy pleasure, he gets whatever he needs because he deserves it. He doesn't need to shop for love because he is part of life; he experiences it from the inside.

The War

World War I ended six years before the novel begins but it continues to affect each of the characters. Jake's genital wound destroyed his hope of romantic fulfillment; the death of a soldier, Brett's first true love, destroyed her capacity for selfless love.

Though the war was unimaginably destructive, it did have an excitement and drama that make postwar life seem drab in comparison. One reason the characters go to the bullfights in Spain is to recapture the excitement of the war. The fiesta is like a battlefield— it catches the characters up in something larger than themselves and lets them forget their own meager lives.

STYLE

After World War I Hemingway felt he had to start over, to learn how to do things simply and truly again. "I was trying to learn to write, commencing with the simplest things," Hemingway said of his life in Paris in the 1920s. He was trying to "put down what I see and what I feel in the best and simplest way I can tell it." To accomplish this, Hemingway banished all literary frills from his writing. *The Sun Also Rises*, for instance, contains almost no metaphors or similes, very few adjectives, and even fewer adverbs. Hemingway wanted to focus on "things" in themselves, and so he used only simple nouns, and simple verbs. His style, compared to the style of many other writers you have read, is extremely lean.

Hemingway also believed that if a writer knew his subject well enough, he did not need to write everything he knew. Writing, to him, was like the tip of an iceberg; the reader would see only one-eighth but would feel and understand the rest.

Hemingway further believed that he could reach his readers through the physical and emotional reactions of his characters. By lucidly describing sensations—smells, sights, sounds—he hoped to produce the same feelings in his readers.

The Sun Also Rises is not simply a dramatic story of love and betrayal, nor is it only a travelog or an allegory of damnation and salvation—though it's all of these things in part. It is also Hemingway's effort to put his theory of writing into practice. Robert Cohn, who blubbers self-consciously, doesn't have good style in life or in writing (his novel was bad). The bullfighter Pedro Romero, on the other hand, has terrific style: if he wrote as he fights bulls, his style would be like Hemingway's—clean, enduringly pure, and professional. He would get the job done economically. He would avoid tricks or mystification; he would never show off. Thus when Hemingway celebrates Romero's bullfighting technique, he is indirectly celebrating his own writing style.

Hemingway broke with writing styles of the past. Popular writing before him generally was florid and overwritten, sentimental and loaded with compound sentences. Hemingway may not have been the first to use a simpler style (that other American expatriate in Paris, Gertrude Stein, always believed that Hemingway copied her style and made a fortune from it), but he was the first to enjoy critical success with it, and he radically changed the public's taste in fiction. Immediately after the publication of *The Sun Also Rises* numerous writers began to mimic him.

POINT OF VIEW

The events in *The Sun Also Rises* are described through the eyes of Jake Barnes, so you have to look carefully at Jake's strengths and weaknesses in order to judge how reliable he is as a narrator.

Do not mistake Jake for Hemingway. Jake is a fully realized character created by the author; he does not necessarily say everything that Hemingway believes. There may have been some superficial similarities between Hemingway and Jake: they were the same age, both were journalists in Paris, both were Americans, and both were wounded during World War I, although in different ways. But they should never be taken for the same person.

Jake is what is called an "unreliable narrator." He tells the story, but he tells you only what he wants you to know, sometimes putting himself in a good light, other times not. He also makes judgments about characters with which you might not agree. His hatred of Robert Cohn, for example, is colored by his jealousy and anger over Cohn's affair with Brett. He also has endless tolerance for Mike Campbell who, at least when you see him in the novel, is nothing but a drunken, obnoxious anti-Semite. As a reader, you have to decide for yourself what you think of Cohn, Mike, and all the other characters. Making up your own mind about them is not only your right, it is a way of participating creatively in the novel.

Though you may find yourself not liking Jake, he's the only one telling the story, so you have to trust him for basic facts. In weighing his judgments, keep in mind his prejudices, such as his dislike of American tourists, and his respect for people with what he calls *afición* (passion).

FORM AND STRUCTURE

The Sun Also Rises is divided into three distinct sections.

Part I, set in Paris, introduces the major characters and their relationships. In Part II we follow them on a trip to Spain. Bill and Jake go fishing in the Spanish countryside, then join the others at Pamplona, a small town that holds a yearly bullfight festival. Part III is an epilog following the fiesta. The book ends in another large city, Madrid.

The three sections can be seen as a series of movements: from city to country to city, and from wasteland to bountiful land to wasteland. Jake moves from sickness to health (on his fishing trip) and back to sickness. Brett descends into her own private hell, wallows in it, then through her one moral act, demonstrates the possibility of salvation.

The Story

BOOK I

CHAPTER I

The first chapter is a portrait of Robert Cohn, drawn by his friend (and the book's narrator) Jake Barnes. Keep in mind that Jake Barnes is not Hemingway, nor is he always completely reliable as a narrator. Jake has very strong beliefs that can cloud his judgment, so you should not trust everything he tells you. Robert Cohn is a good case in point: Jake makes him out to be the book's villain, but don't blindly accept this. Some readers consider Cohn the hero of the book.

Robert Cohn comes from a wealthy Jewish family. He went to Princeton at a time when the school was filled with socially prominent white Anglo-Saxons. As a Jew, he was made to feel like an outsider. Too shy and gentle to attack the school's anti-Semitism straight on, he turned to boxing and became the school's middleweight champion. This was his only success, and years later none of his classmates even remembers him.

NOTE: At school Cohn developed a "painful self-consciousness," probably because he could never forget he was a Jew and an outsider. Self-consciousness is seen by Jake and his friends as a sign of weakness. They have no patience or sympathy for a person who is easily ruffled and who cannot distance himself from his feelings. To Jake and the others, it's better to know who you are and to accept yourself without apologies or regrets. Cohn, on the contrary, is always blind to his faults. His blindness gets him and others into trouble.

Rejected at school, Cohn married "the first girl who was nice to him." The marriage came to nothing, and just when Cohn decided to leave her, she beat him to it. Even life itself, it seemed, was unable to take Cohn seriously, and treated him as a joke.

Doing the fashionable thing, Cohn now became involved in the arts, first as a patron, then by starting his own magazine. This put him in the company of other writers, which made him feel he ought to write a novel. He did, but it was poor.

Jake now brings us up to the present. Cohn has become involved with a woman named Frances, and has gone off to Paris with her. Many young Americans—including Jake—are living here after World War I.

NOTE: The Bohemian life-style of these expatriate Americans is in many ways the subject of the book. Notice how their days are spent doing nothing but sitting in cafés, eating and drinking, talking about writing, and gossiping about people and their affairs.

It is in a café that Jake finds out how tight a rein Frances keeps on Cohn. When Jake suggests they go to Austria—Jake knows a girl there who can show them around—Cohn kicks him under the table. Frances is fiercely jealous. Cohn, a victim of his need for acceptance, is afraid to upset her, and refuses to go.

Jake, it seems, is fond of Robert Cohn, but he feels sorry for him, too.

CHAPTER II

Jake tells about Cohn's trip to America, where his new book is favorably received. Women are suddenly attracted to him, and both successes go to his head.

Cohn starts to look at other women, and Frances feels rightly threatened.

NOTE: By now you should have learned something important about Cohn and his relationship to the other characters in the book. Cohn is an old-fashioned romantic. The others are realists; they see the world as it is. Cohn, according to Jake, sees life falsely because he sees it as he would like it to be. Cohn, for instance, thinks life is "pretty." Jake ridicules him for getting his ideas from books, and not even good books at that. One, *The Purple Land*, tells of "splendid imaginary amorous adventures . . . in an intensely romantic land." Later you'll watch Cohn pursue a woman (who he wrongly believes loves him) to the supposedly romantic land of Spain.

Cohn begs Jake to run off with him to South America. If anything sounds like an impossibly romantic adventure, this surely does—and Jake of course refuses to go. So what if you're not leading the life of a hero, he tells Cohn, "nobody ever lives their life all the way up except bull-fighters."

Cohn keeps after Jake, and Jake uses a ploy to get rid of him. He invites Cohn to a café beneath the newspaper office where Jake works, buys him a drink, then says he has to get back to work. Even this doesn't get rid of Cohn, who falls alseep outside the office. Cohn, here and elsewhere, seems a tagalong, a younger brother who wants to go everywhere, even when his older brother wants to be left alone.

Jake, the realistic voice, tells Cohn that a person can't escape himself: "You can't get away from yourself by moving from one place to another," he says. Jake believes that a person should live with himself, hard as that may be. Cohn, on the contrary, wants to be someone other than himself. As a reader you can share Jake's belief that Cohn's blindness to himself is a fault; or you can see this blindness as a strength, giving Cohn a sense of purpose and a capacity for sacrifice that the "realistic" characters lack.

How does a person with no illusions learn to live with himself? Jake, named after the Biblical Jacob who wrestled the angel one long night, spends his life wrestling with this question without ever resolving it.

CHAPTER III

Now that we know Robert Cohn—that he has been an outsider all his life, and that women can dominate him—the book's focus turns to Jake Barnes. It's twilight, and Jake takes a seat in a café to watch *poules* (chicks; that is, girls) walk past. A prostitute named Georgette struts by, catches Jake's eye, then joins him.

Georgette, as a streetwalker, has seen a lot of life, and she knows how to talk tough. She's one of the realists, without illusions. She doesn't hesitate to invite herself to have dinner with Jake, and in the taxi she lowers her hand to his lap. But he pushes her hand away.

Here we learn one of the most important things about Jake: he has a wound that has damaged his genitalia. We never learn exactly what the wound is, but we do know that it keeps him from making love, although it doesn't stop him from feeling desire. The wound torments Jake: whenever he wants a woman he must face the fact that he can do nothing about it.

NOTE: Many readers see Jake as a symbol of life in the years after World War I. They liken him to the mythological character, a part of many legends including that of Perceval and Gawain, called generically the Fisher King. The Fisher King became impotent and then his kingdom became impotent, too. When he regained his potency, his kingdom blossomed. Jake's sterility, like the Fisher King's is also the sterility of the world. He cannot love, and there is almost no love in the world he lives in. Some readers see the book as Jake's quest to become personally healthy and to heal the world. Watch to see if he has any success.

When Georgette says, after hearing about his wound, "Everybody's sick. I'm sick, too," you're meant to make this connection between Jake and those around him. The war has undermined everyone's optimism and destroyed everyone's hope and faith. The world seems a sterile place, with no permanent values and no fine human emotions. Some readers call this postwar world a wasteland, after T. S. Eliot's poem, "The Waste Land," published four years before *The Sun Also Rises.* Used here, "wasteland" means a world in which things seems sick, impotent, and sterile.

At dinner Jake and Georgette discuss the war. Jake calls it a "calamity for civilization."

NOTE: World War I was a great historical cataclysm that changed the mood of many people from one of simple hopefulness to one of complicated and

frustrated despair. It's important to remember that
The Sun Also Rises takes place only six years after Armistice Day, the day ending the war, and that the war is still on everyone's mind. Some of the characters miss the excitement of the war; others, like Jake, have never recovered from what the war did to them.

Jake had thought he'd enjoy eating with a prostitute more than he does, so he's pleased when an old friend, an American writer named Braddocks, drags him and Georgette to a *bal musette*, a risqué nightclub.

Lady Brett Ashley, the book's heroine, arrives at the club surrounded by a group of young male homosexuals. She's a 34-year-old Englishwoman who became titled when she married her second husband, from whom she's now separated. She's thin and beautiful, yet her short hair, like her name itself, gives her a masculine air.

Brett smokes and drinks, has careless affairs with men, runs around with homosexuals, and generally acts with blithe irresponsibility. She is very attractive, though, and has a power to draw men around her. Later you'll see her referred to as a festival goddess, and also as Circe, the Greek mythological figure who tempted men and then turned them into swine. An important question to ask yourself is whether Brett is an evil figure like Circe or just a sad, aging woman.

Jake hates homosexuals; his first impulse is to "swing [at] one, any one." Some people think that men who want to strike out at homosexuals are worried about their own manliness. Certainly, with his wound, a good case can be made that Jake is afraid he's not enough of a man.

NOTE: Manliness—defined at its best by courage, strength, and clearheadedness, and at its worst
by pigheadedness, random brutality, and violence—
is a quality most of the male characters in the book
worry about. Jake is physically less than a man.
Another character you'll meet, Mike Campbell, seems
obsessed by the need to prove his masculinity. Some
readers think the Hemingway hero, with his macho
poses, is no more than a comic-book figure. Others
argue that Hemingway's heroes are too three-dimen-
sional to be reduced to any one characteristic.

Everyone gets drunk. Throughout the book when
people get together they drink. Gallons of liquor are
consumed in *The Sun Also Rises*. This is one way the
characters rebel against society's prohibitions back
home. It is also a way of pouring pleasure into otherwise empty lives. Jake, watching from the bar, says,
"This whole show makes me sick." Though he is part
of the scene, he is also disgusted by what passes for
civilization around him.

Robert Cohn appears and falls instantly in love with
Brett. He asks Brett to dance, but she's with Jake.

When Jake leaves with Brett, he leaves money for
Georgette. He's thoughtful enough to realize that
even if he can't use her full services as a prostitute, he
has taken up her time. In a taxi Brett turns to Jake and
tells him, "I've been so miserable." We'll find out
what's bothering her in the next chapter.

CHAPTER IV

Brett says, "Don't touch me," when Jake tries to
kiss her. It seems she doesn't want to get involved
with him, yet the truth is more complicated. Jake and

Brett have loved each other and are still physically attracted to each other. "I simply turn all to jelly when you touch me," Brett says. But they can't do anything about their desire; they can't consummate their love because of Jake's wound. There is another reason, too: they are in the wasteland, where, as Brett says, "Love is hell on earth."

Their predicament is ironic, Brett feels. "When I think of the hell I've put chaps through," she says. "I'm paying for it now." After hurting so many men she couldn't love, she's now being hurt by a man who can't love her.

Jake tries to joke about his wound, and to convince Brett that he never gives it much thought. Brett knows better. But Jake, in his tough-guy manner, can't let on that he's disturbed. His incapacity obviously colors his whole life, and the more he tries to forget it, the more he becomes obsessed by it.

Although Brett and Jake realize their love is impossible, they need each other too much to stay apart for long. Brett, we learn, has been wounded emotionally earlier in life, and she and Jake, sharing their sense of loss, understand each other only too well.

At the *bal musette* Jake is introduced to Count Mippipopolous, a pudgy, excessively polite Greek and older friend of Brett's. We'll see later on how this man made his own bargain with the hopelessness of postwar Europe.

Jake and Brett set a date to meet the next day, and Jake heads home. Alone in his apartment, his tough-guy front begins to fall apart. His thoughts keep turning to Brett. "To hell with Brett," he thinks. Their impossible situation only makes him angry, but he can't think of anything else.

NOTE: Self-control is an important quality of the "Hemingway Code" of manly behavior. In public, Jake tries to appear cool and unruffled. But we see him as none of the other characters do: when he's alone. It's sad to see how when he's not in the company of others he loses his self-control.

Nights are not easy for Jake. (Later we learn that for six months after he was wounded he slept with a nightlight.) The war had reduced him to a frightened child. His thoughts are confused. He can't sleep. He's bitter about his wound; he's also angry that he has insomnia. The Catholic Church has advised him not to think about his wound, but such advice is not much help. Still capable of feeling sadness, at least, he breaks down and cries.

At 4:30 Jake is awakened by Brett, who has been driving around with Count Mippipopolous, and wants to know if Jake will join them. He's not interested. Brett tells Jake that the count is "one of us." The count has offered Brett $10,000 to run off with him to the French beach resort of Biarritz. She declines. She's in love with Jake, she says, and then she's off again to spend the rest of the night driving around Paris with the count.

Jake has only one thing to say about his life at this point: "It is awfully easy to be hard-boiled about everything in the daytime, but at night it is another thing." What Jake means in effect is that it's easy to fool other people about oneself, but it's not so easy to fool oneself.

CHAPTER V

In the morning the sun is shining. Jake feels better and enjoys a pleasant walk to work. He's a journalist, and off to report a speech. When he returns to his office, Robert Cohn is there. Cohn asks Jake to lunch, not simply to be friendly but because he wants to pump Jake for information about Brett. He says he might be in love with her.

Jake tells Cohn that he met Brett when he was a patient in the hospital. She was a V.A.D., a volunteer nurse's aide. She had a "true love" then, but he died of dysentery. Brett shared Cohn's belief in romance then, but losing her lover made her bitter.

When Cohn says, "I don't believe she would marry anybody she didn't love," Jake points out, "She's done it twice." But Cohn refuses to accept the truth; truth has no place in his fantasy. He becomes abusive to Jake and then quickly apologizes to keep his friend. Poor Cohn: he considers Jake the best friend he has. "God help you," Jake thinks, pitying him.

But Jake feels something more than pity, something that verges on jealously or anger toward the man who is about to make a pass at the woman he loves. Yet he can't believe Cohn will have any success with her.

CHAPTER VI

Jake is waiting for Brett at a posh hotel. To pass the time he's writing a letter.

NOTE: When Jake writes, "They were not very good letters but I hoped their being on Crillon stationery would help them," he is saying that it's easy to deceive by putting a fancy label on something that is less than satisfactory. Appearances can belie the truth. This theme of truth versus appearances will be very important when we watch the bullfighters in action.

Brett stands Jake up, and Jake takes a taxi to a Left Bank café where he meets Harvey Stone, yet another expatriate American writer.

NOTE: According to a joke of the 1920s, if you threw a rock in the air on the Left Bank of Paris (the artists' district) you'd bean an American would-be writer. Jake and Stone talk about H. L. Mencken, the American writer, editor, and social critic who was influential in the 1920s. Mencken was an iconoclast, and his barbs against the American middle class were picked up by the young Americans who went to Paris to live the life of Bohemian artists. Stone says that Mencken's all written out, implying that young Americans need a new figure to "set their likes and dislikes." Interestingly, Ernest Hemingway challenged Mencken's place with the publication of *The Sun Also Rises*. After its publication Americans at home and abroad began talking tough-guy talk like Jake and his friends; Jake and Brett were heroes for thousands. Their effect on young people's attitudes was not much different from that of rock stars today— they influenced dress, social behavior, and ideas.

Robert Cohn turns up and Stone asks him jokingly what he'd do with his life if he could do anything. Cohn would like to play football again. It's an impossible, even sad wish, and Stone calls Cohn a "case of arrested development." Cohn, unable to tolerate criticism, says somebody should beat Stone up. Both men behave like children pushing each other around on a school playground.

Frances, Cohn's fiancée, comes to their table and drags Jake away to a café across the street to talk to him in private.

Cohn is leaving her, she announces to Jake. When she begins to whine, Jake says, "There's no use talking about it, is there?" Talking too much about what you can't change is not part of the "code."

Back with Cohn, Frances accuses him of sending her to England to get rid of her. (This is true; he doesn't want her in the way while he pursues Brett.) Frances begins to insult Cohn mercilessly and Cohn, to Jake's bewilderment, simply takes it. Is he too weak to defend himself? Is he unwilling to argue because he knows she is right? Or is it possible that living by his own romantic code he refuses to be abusive to a woman? Hemingway never tells us. Perhaps Cohn, as a Jew and an outsider, has gotten used to being abused: it defines him and gives him a sense of who he is. In any case, he can afford to ignore her since she will be leaving soon, freeing him to pursue Brett.

Jake can't take any more of Frances and Cohn. He slips away with a lie, and takes a taxi home.

CHAPTER VII

Brett and Count Mippipopolous visit Jake at his apartment. Brett wants to be alone with Jake, and sends the count off for champagne.

Do Brett and Jake try to make love again? There are gaps in the narrative—almost like frames edited from a movie—so it's hard to tell. In any case, Jake feels desperate and asks Brett if they couldn't live together. Brett can only answer, "I don't think so. I'd just *tromper* you with everybody. You couldn't stand it." (*Tromper* is a French word meaning to cheat or deceive.)

To prove that she can't be trusted she tells Jake that she's going away for a while—to San Sebastian in northern Spain. Jake wants to go with her, but she says he can't. She doesn't admit it, but she's going with someone else. A perceptive reader can probably guess with whom.

Back comes the count, loaded down with champagne. He has his own code, his own set of what he calls "values," and he tells Jake and Brett about it.

Titles don't count for anything, he says; it's not whether you're a count or a princess that matters, but simply who you are. He also never plays people false. "Joke people and you make enemies," he says. The count's philosophy is to be straightforward with others.

Brett, unlike the count, plays false with others, and she says she has no friends except Jake. Why Jake? Because she is always honest with him. Their honesty, in fact, is their strongest bond.

Corks pop. The count's champagne is "amazing." When he spends money, he gets only the best. Brett calls him "one of us."

NOTE: "One of us," to these expatriates, means being experienced, and having a wound, like a badge, to prove it. We already know about Jake's wound. What is Brett's? Evidently the way she has been treated by men. And the count's? He shows us, raising his shirt on "two raised white welts." He was shot by an arrow in Abyssinia (Ethiopia) years before. His is a very classy merit badge, proof that he belongs in the clique.

The count's value system is based on knowing what one should pay to get the most pleasure for one's money. He has no illusions that the pleasures of life are free, and is willing to pay liberally for everything he wants. In his pursuit of pleasure the count is similar to Jake and Brett. But although these values satisfy the count, they do not seem enough for the younger, more restless expatriates, or at least not for Jake and Brett, who are still trying to give some lasting meaning to their lives. Is the count really "one of us," as Brett says? Although the Americans who came to Paris after the war were turning their backs on the strict morality of prewar America and learning to enjoy pleasure for its own sake, they hadn't given up their search for truth. Such a search seems to be beyond the count's simple pursuit of pleasure.

In his typically lean style, Hemingway does not spell out the differences between the count's and Jake's value systems. You are left to decide what might be missing in the count's life, whether he has forfeited spontaneity, religion, permanent values, and profound love for a more comfortable system of trading upward in personal pleasure.

The count orders a bottle of 1811 brandy, the oldest in the house. Brett protests, but he insists. Nothing at that moment would give him more pleasure. We wonder if the brandy is being wasted on Jake and Brett, who demand different kinds of pleasure. Hemingway leaves us to answer such questions for ourselves.

After dinner the three of them go to a nightclub, where suddenly Jake feels terrible:

> I had the feeling as in a nightmare of it all being something repeated, something I had been through and that now I must go through again.

What is being repeated are the endless, pointless rounds of drinking and dancing. Jake needs a vacation. And so Book I ends. In Book II the group will leave behind the decadent and tiresome thrills of Paris for the purer pleasures of Spain.

BOOK II

CHAPTER VIII

With Brett and Robert Cohn away, Jake's life quiets. Then his old friend Bill Gorton arrives from the States. Bill is another writer (a successful one), and another drunk. He has just come to Paris after a long binge in Austria.

Bill is also a talker and a compulsive joker. Though he can be funny, often he's very cruel. Gifted as he is with words, he scatters them at times like machine-gun fire, caring little for whom or what he hits.

Jake, who's more careful with his words, nevertheless enjoys talking with Bill and trying to play his game. And sometimes Bill says telling things about himself and about the world he lives in.

Once, when they're walking by a taxidermist's shop, Bill asks Jake if he wants a stuffed dog. "Simple exchange of values," Bill says. "You give them money. They give you a stuffed dog."

NOTE: Bill's words should remind you of the count and his value system. Bill unwittingly parodies it. At least the count knows value; Bill, however, is willing to spend his money on something as worthless as a stuffed dog. The count is right about one thing: when you shop in the wasteland you do well if you get anything at all of value. But love, faith, abundant life—can they be bought?

Walking the streets, Jake and Bill bump into Brett, just back from Spain.

NOTE: Brett says she must have a bath. This is certainly not an unusual wish after a long trip, but Brett often remarks that she needs a bath. This is symbolic of her need to cleanse herself spiritually. Having just returned from a tryst with Jake's friend Robert Cohn, she may want to wash away a sense of sin, or at least an unpleasant experience. For the corrupt, water is a symbol of renewal. Do they ever get truly cleansed? It doesn't seem so, at least not so that it lasts.

Even Bill falls for Brett, but when he hears she's engaged, he backs off. Bill has a better sense than Robert Cohn of where he belongs and where he doesn't.

The three characters wind up at Madame Lecomte's restaurant, a place where they've dined before, but not since it was written up in an American guidebook. Now it's crowded with American tourists. Jake and Bill resent finding themselves surrounded by the very people they had come to Europe to escape.

NOTE: Though Jake and his friends are expatriates and familiar with European ways, they are really tourists themselves. Tourists keep appearing in the novel, reminding these members of the Lost Generation that they themselves are eternal tourists without homelands, onlookers instead of participants in life. Their sense of being outside of life looking in will be made more acute in Spain, where they remain strangers to the closed culture and to the rituals of the bullfight.

After dinner Jake and Bill stroll through Paris. This long description of Parisian life has little to do with the action of the novel. The beauty of Paris, though, makes an impression on Bill, and for the first time he turns down a drink.

Finally they arrive at the Rotonde café where they meet Brett and her newly arrived fiancé, Mike Campbell. Mike is a Scot, and by his own admission a notorious drunk and bankrupt. He is also a vicious anti-Semite—you'll see him constantly refer to Robert Cohn as "little Jew." He even speaks disparagingly of Brett, saying in his drunken and rambling way, "I say, Brett, you *are* a lovely piece." And yet Mike is accepted by Jake and the others. What makes him more acceptable than Cohn? For one thing, he's not Jewish. But the ways of the "in crowd" are often mysterious, and you'll have to decide for yourself why Mike is accepted. By the end of the chapter we can see that Mike is as dominated by women as Robert Cohn is. When Jake and Bill invite Mike to a boxing match, he doesn't think Brett would want him to go, so he declines.

NOTE: As you read *The Sun Also Rises*, take note of the similarities among characters, how one reminds you of another. There is·some of Cohn in Jake and Mike, some of Brett in Jake, and a little of Jake in the bullfighter Pedro Romero. In some ways the characters are parodies of each other; in other ways, they complement each other.

CHAPTER IX

The next day Jake tells Brett and Mike about the trip to Spain he's planning. First he and Bill will go fishing in Burguete, then on to Pamplona, an inland Basque town with a famous fiesta called the *Feria del San Fermín*, complete with a running of the bulls through the city streets and a week of bullfights. Robert Cohn has already been invited; now Mike asks if he and Brett can go. Jake says that would be grand.

After Mike leaves, Brett drops a bombshell: it was Robert Cohn with whom she went to San Sebastian. Jake feels as though somebody's kicked his chest in, but remains calm. Remember, it's easy to be hard-boiled in the daylight.

Brett worries about Cohn coming to Spain: it will be difficult enough being with both her fiancé Mike and her "true love" Jake. She writes to Cohn to give him a chance to pull out, but he doesn't take the hint. Cohn never seems to know when he's not wanted.

On the train from Paris Jake and Bill share a compartment with a good-humored American family, and listen to the wife scoffing at the way her husband drinks when he goes on fishing trips with his buddies. Through this family we glimpse the small-town, American world that these expatriates have gone to Europe to escape. (Whether the life of these expatriates is richer and more rewarding than the life of this typical American family is something you should think about.)

Many American pilgrims are traveling in the train from Rome to Lourdes, a town where the waters of a spring are believed to bring miraculous cures. You can imagine how two notorious iconoclasts like Jake and Bill feel about such believers. Jake says he's a Roman Catholic, too, though an unhappy one. Earlier in the novel, when he was alone at night thinking about his wound, he lamented that the Catholic Church could do nothing to help him. Now we learn that Jake wants to believe in Catholicism but can't. He feels let down and bitter over the church's failure to help him. Jake hurts not only because of his wound, but because all his former beliefs have deserted him. Without the church he feels helplessly alone. Bill, in contrast, cares nothing about the church except as a target for his wisecracks.

CHAPTER X

There's no bus to Pamplona, so they have to hire a car and driver.

NOTE: Now that the characters are out of the city, the style of writing changes. Hemingway uses his simple, rhythmic, descriptive style—he said he learned it from looking at how Cézanne painted landscapes, with a wide brush full of subtle, muted shades.

The country has a peaceful, relaxing effect that is captured in sentences like this: "It was hot, but the town had a cool, fresh, early-morning smell and it was pleasant sitting in the café." Note how Hemingway avoids figures of speech and metaphors, and limits himself to general physical impressions. Doesn't this sentence make you feel you're sitting outside, with your shoes off, on a warm, beautiful summer day? As you read, compare descriptions of the fresh, clean Spanish countryside with earlier descriptions of life in the city. The countryside has something healing about it, even for Jake.

Jake, Bill, and Cohn arrive in Pamplona and meet Montoya, the owner of the Hotel Montoya. (Montoya, as you will see, knows the old, enduring values, and finally comes to judge Jake harshly by them.) The three Americans enjoy a bountiful lunch (nature overflows with goodness in Spain). Cohn doesn't believe Brett and Mike will arrive that night, and he voices his doubts in a way that irks Bill. Out of anger, Bill foolishly makes a bet with Cohn that he then realizes he'll lose.

After lunch Jake goes off for a walk around town and enters the cathedral. He kneels and starts to pray for everybody and everything he can think of. It's a rambling prayer, and suddenly he becomes self-conscious about it and grows a bit ashamed: "I . . . regretted that I was such a rotten Catholic, but realized there was nothing I could do about it, at least for a while, and maybe never, but that anyway it was a grand religion, and I only wished I felt religious and maybe would the next time. . . . " Jake tries to remain honest with himself—his self-esteem depends on it. Self-honesty is one of the few things he can hold onto and believe in in this fallen world. Jake still remembers how life before the war was guided by tradition and belief, and he knows only too well how far he and his friends have strayed from that life. As you'll see, Montoya knows, too.

At dinner Cohn is nervous about Brett's arrival, and Jake goes to the railroad station with him. But Brett and Mike aren't on the train; Cohn has won the bet. He says he doesn't want the money. Can he bet on bullfights? Bill says he can but he shouldn't: the point of a bullfight is not to bet as you bet on a horse race, but to experience the purer pleasure of watching how it's done.

A telegram arrives: Brett and Mike are stopping in San Sebastian. The mention of that town makes Jake think of Brett and Cohn's affair there, and his composure melts. "I was blind, unforgivingly jealous of what had happened to him," he says, and who can blame him? Another man went away with the woman he loves, and he can do nothing about it. Jake's simple annoyance at Cohn is beginning to grow into jealousy.

The next day Cohn bows out of the fishing trip with Jake and Bill; he thinks Brett is expecting him in San Sebastian. Brett is with her fiancé, but Cohn, holding onto his romantic notion of love, believes that since Brett once slept with him, she will love him forever, no matter who else she's with. Jake, thinking Cohn is gloating over the affair, hates him all the more, though he's too self-controlled to abuse Cohn in public. Bill is just as glad as Jake that Cohn's not going fishing with them, for Cohn would probably spend the whole time blathering about his immature feelings.

CHAPTER XI

Jake and Bill board a crowded bus to Burguete, where a lovely camaraderie develops between the Americans and the Spaniards. A big leather wine bag is passed around. The peasants are generous and uncomplicated; they want nothing in return. Neither city life nor the war has destroyed their simple enjoyment of life.

The Spanish countryside suddenly opens on a "green valley," like a vision of Eden. A stream goes through the center of town, and fields of grapes touch the houses. The cares of the city seem to fall away as Jake and Bill reach an inn high in the mountains, near the Irati River, where they will fish the next day. At first they think the proprietress is overcharging. But they needn't be suspicious; wine is included with the room. They eat and go to bed. "It felt good to be warm and in bed," says Jake, and we have to ask ourselves, is this the same man who was tortured by insomnia only days ago, back in Paris?

CHAPTER XII

The next morning Jake wakes up early and goes out to dig worms for the fishing trip. Bill wants Jake to be ironical but Jake can't. Now that he's in Spain he wants everything simple and straightforward. (To be ironical is to make fun of things, something the count said one shouldn't do.)

Bill, unable to get Jake to be ironical with him, knocks him for being an expatriate.

> You're an expatriate. You've lost touch with the soil. You get precious. Fake European standards have ruined you. You drink yourself to death. You become obsessed by sex. You spend all your time talking, not working. You are an expatriate, see? You hang around cafés.

Bill is half-joking here, and Jake accepts all the criticism except that about his commitment to his work. He can't joke about that at all.

NOTE: Notice how Hemingway's male characters avoid intimate or emotional conversations. The Hemingway hero handles his emotional burdens alone. For Jake it would be repulsive to speak to Bill about his impotence. Robert Cohn, who will confess his innermost feelings to anyone who will listen, is one of Hemingway's antiheroes.

Jake and Bill hike to the Irati River to fish. The falls are simply jumping with trout.

NOTE: The river teeming with fish is a symbol of fertility, an antidote to the sterile wasteland of the modern city. Jake, as Fisher King, is right at home. The fish are even easy to catch. Jake simply baits his hook and the fish grab it. The fish themselves are beautiful, cool, and firm. Everything is perfect.

Jake reads a book, a fanciful tale of a man who has fallen into a glacier, and the woman who is going to wait 24 years for him to unfreeze. Some readers see this as an ironic comment on "true love": the person who waits for it never gets anything.

Bill mentions at lunch that Bryan died yesterday. He's referring to William Jennings Bryan, the famous politician and orator who fought against the right to teach evolutionary theory. Notice, when he makes fun of Bryan's beliefs, how Bill always has to be "on," always has to poke fun at someone or something. He seems able to stand only by crushing the rest of the world beneath him.

CHAPTER XIII

Jake and Bill head back to Pamplona. Cohn, Brett, and Mike have already arrived.

Montoya, the innkeeper, and Jake talk about bulls and *afición*. *Afición* means passion, and an *aficionado* is one who is passionate about the bullfights. *Afición* is a special quality. Not every bullfighter has it. The pictures of those with *afición* Montoya frames; the others he keeps in a drawer or throws out. Their inscriptions are full of flattery. Why? Probably because these men have to say with words what bullfighters with *afición* say with themselves, with their gestures. Note that Hemingway uses language in the same way that men with *afición* fight bulls—with precision and economy. Neither is interested in showing off.

The *aficionados* come from all over to stay at Montoya's; they're always treated well. They form a brotherhood. Only one of the Americans has *afición*—Jake

Barnes. How do the Spaniards know? Not by asking directly, but indirectly, by watching him. Montoya, a man with traditional values, forgives Jake for having shameful friends like Brett, Mike, Bill, and Robert Cohn. Why? Because Jake has *afición*.

Bill and Jake talk about how steers are used to keep the bulls from fighting each other. When the bulls are let out of their cages the steers "run around like old maids trying to quiet them down."

NOTE: Some readers see the bulls and steers as symbols for some of the characters. Which are bulls—active, domineering, courageous? Probably only Pedro Romero. And which are steers? Probably Jake, Robert Cohn, and Mike.

At lunch Mike tells the others a story about how he rented some war medals from his tailor before a dinner with the Prince of Wales. The Prince didn't show up, and Mike had no other need for the medals, so he gave them to friends. The tailor wanted them back because they belonged to other clients who had earned them and who valued them. None of the men at the table has any sympathy for those who lost the medals. They know too much of the horror of war to believe in honor or glory. In their eyes, World War I made heroes of no one.

After eating they go to watch the unloading of the bulls. Brett has told Mike about her affair with Cohn. What makes Mike mad, however, is not her infidelity—he's used to that—but the fact that Cohn doesn't know that Brett's now finished with him. Cohn's romantic sense of absolutes—absolute love, absolute commitment—goes against Mike's grain. Not man enough to fight Cohn, Mike taunts him, calling him a steer for following Brett around all the time.

NOTE: What is Brett's power over men? Sexual, certainly, but more than that: she is a goddess of the wasteland. Men don't simply love her, they worship her. In a way she has replaced the religion that no longer works for Jake and his friends.

At dinner differences are put aside. Everybody behaves. The meal reminds Jake of times during the war when "there was much wine, an ignored tension, and a feeling of things coming that you could not prevent happening." Jake is implying here that wine, like war, induces a feeling that events are beyond our personal control.

NOTE: The idea of being carried away by forces outside his control seems attractive to Jake, as it would be to anyone who has difficulty handling emotional complications. Jake's life is in disorder; one reason he looks forward to the fiesta is that everybody will be wild and crazy and he can simply lose himself in the excitement of the moment.

CHAPTER XIV

Jake goes to bed that night very drunk. He hears Brett laughing in a nearby room with another man, and he starts to break down again. For six months he has never slept with the light off, and he's afraid to turn it off now—he's afraid of the dark. He curses Brett, but his real problem is his impotence.

"Enjoying living was learning to get your money's worth and knowing when you had it," he says, recalling Count Mippipopolous' philosophy. He hopes this thought will comfort him. But then he adds, "In five years . . . it will seem just as silly as all the other fine philosophies I've had."

NOTE: Or will it? One of the issues in *The Sun Also Rises* is whether a person can get closer to the meaning of life as he gets older, whether he can become wiser, or whether each of us goes through life simply trying on one "philosophy" after another, all ultimately worthless. Maybe a person does learn something, Jake thinks, not in any ultimate sense, but in the practical sense of learning how to live in the world. Jake doesn't want deep philosophy; he just wants something that works. Does he find it? He refines his values throughout the book, but by the end he has also made huge mistakes—with Brett, and with his friend Montoya. We can say this much for him: unlike his friends, he tries to learn. Part of his nobility as a character comes from these private moments when he searches for a better way to live.

CHAPTER XV

A rocket goes up and the fiesta begins. The hurly-burly of the festivities gives the expatriates a sense of excitement they haven't felt since the war. Perhaps that's why the rocket's smoke, hanging in the sky, is compared to a shrapnel burst. Dancers move to the sounds of wild music. The people, needing an icon to worship, turn to Brett: "Brett wanted to dance but they did not want her to. They wanted her as an image to dance around." For a brief, beautiful moment Brett is transformed into a goddess. Caught up in the excitement, she, like the others, becomes whole again, and content. For as long as the festivities last she and her friends can escape into a world of blind revelry and regain a sense of oneness with life that they have lost. Jake describes his mood when he says, "It seemed out of place to think of consequences during the festival." Anything goes, nothing matters, all ethical constraints are lifted. Being at the fiesta feels like freedom, but, as you'll see, it doesn't make anybody feel very good for long. Only working within a framework of responsibility seems able to do that.

Jake wakes from a nap and goes out on the hotel balcony to watch the famous running of the bulls.

NOTE: Each year bulls are turned loose from their cages, and chase a crowd of Spaniards and tourists through the narrow, cobblestoned streets of Pamplona. The buildings are flush against the street, so each street is like a long, tight corridor. Men, trying to prove how macho they are, run in front of the bulls, challenging them, and not all of the men get away unscathed.

This is Brett's first bullfight and she's worried about what she's going to see. The horses that carry picadors—the men who use pics or long lances to prod the bulls when they're not fast enough or angry enough—are often gored to death. The bulls are killed, too, and Brett worries that the blood and violence may be too much for her to handle. Jake says she'll be fine; she can simply turn her head away when the scene gets too bloody.

Robert Cohn says he's not concerned about the blood. His only worry is that he'll be bored. The tension between Mike and Cohn continues to build; we know it has to resolve itself soon.

Montoya introduces Jake and Bill to Pedro Romero, and we finally see the famous bullfighter.

NOTE: Some readers think that Romero is Hemingway's hero because he best exemplifies the manly virtues of Hemingway's code of behavior—bravery, honesty, and passion. Romero is very handsome, very much the image of the bullfighter. The two other bullfighters look mediocre in comparison.

Bill uses binoculars to see if Cohn, sitting across the stadium, is looking bored. He isn't. Bill calls him a "kike," and nobody objects.

NOTE: Anti-Semitism is easily tolerated if not actually enjoyed by most of the characters in the novel. Perhaps that's because *The Sun Also Rises* was written in 1925, well before the German dictator Adolf Hitler began his campaign to exterminate the Jews. Yet the willingness of the expatriates to condone, or at least to remain silent in the face of anti-Semitism, makes them—particularly Mike and Bill—morally suspect. If you try to understand these characters rather than judge them, you can see that they need Cohn as a scapegoat to compensate for the powerlessness of their own lives. Turning Cohn into an outsider gives them a sense that they themselves belong to a private and privileged group, a small gain considering the moral price they must pay.

Cohn, hardly bored, is nearly sick to his stomach at the sight of the bullfight. Reality is more than he can bear.

On the second day of bullfighting Romero is "the whole show." Jake tells Brett what makes him special: he "never made any contortions, always it was straight and pure and natural in line." That is, he was not interested in show; none of his movements was wasted, all he cared about was doing his job. The true *aficionado* loves to watch Romero "because he kept the absolute purity of line in his movements and always quietly and calmly let the horns pass him close each time. He did not have to emphasize their closeness." Other bullfighters put on a show of bravery for the audience that gives the *aficionado* "an unpleasant feeling." Remember Jake writing his letter on the fancy hotel stationery and feeling bad about it? He was using a trick to make his letter look better. Romero gets as close as he can to real danger; he uses no tricks.

Brett, true to her nature, is excited by the spectacle, even when a bull gores a picador's horse. Although she's engaged to Mike, she falls for Romero.

CHAPTER XVI

There are no bullfights today because it's raining, but the fiesta continues in the streets and cafés.

Montoya tells Jake that the American ambassador has invited Pedro Romero for coffee after dinner. Should Romero go? Montoya is worried that Romero, still only a young man, will be corrupted if he mixes with sophisticated, moneyed people. He's pleased when Jake tells him not to deliver the invitation to Romero.

Jake joins his friends in the hotel dining room, where Bill, drunk, is paying every shoeshine boy he can catch to polish Mike's shoes. Mike, also drunk, plays along. There's a sort of slapstick comedy to the antics of these two men, but there's also very little grace or grandeur.

Pedro Romero asks Jake over to his table. Brett asks to be introduced, too. If she really is Circe, drawing men toward her and corrupting them, we can now see her at work. Montoya, who was worried about Romero meeting the wrong kind of people, starts to smile at Jake, then drops the smile and leaves without even a nod. He obviously feels that Jake is betraying him by letting Brett pursue Romero.

In the meantime Mike has turned on Cohn again, taunting him with more drunken, anti-Semitic remarks. No one interferes. Mike begs Cohn to go away and leave him and Brett alone, but Cohn stands his ground. A romantic fool, he's "ready to do battle for his lady love." The only problem is that Brett's unwilling to play the role. The tension between Mike and Cohn builds, and they come just short of blows.

Out in the plaza fire balloons are going up. These are paper balloons set on fire; as they climb into the blue-black night sky, they burn like small suns. "Globos illuminados," Mike calls them, lit-up balls.

NOTE: Some readers see Hemingway punning here on the physical preoccupations of his male characters. Jake, we remember, cannot have sex. Mike and Cohn try to prove their masculinity by standing up to each other. "Globos illuminados" means, in effect, manly courage, power, passion *(afición)*, and an ability to get things done cleanly and well. Only Pedro Romero seems fully to possess these powers.

At the café Bill has picked up an American girl named Edna. Brett rudely dismisses Cohn so she can talk privately with Jake. Again they condemn Cohn. "He's behaved very badly," Jake says. But what has Cohn done? Nothing much more than to insist in believing in love. Cohn believes that love is worth suffering over, and this infuriates the nonbelievers. It seems sad, doesn't it, that the one American who believes in love is condemned by the others. Yet Cohn, because he's somewhat foolish and out of touch with reality, is hardly worthy of carrying the banner of true love. He *does* behave badly. The problem is that Jake condemns him not only for what's bad about him, but for what is hopeful and good.

NOTE: In condemning Cohn, Jake is also condemning himself, for the two are very much alike. As Jake admits, if he were in Cohn's shoes, he'd be "as big an ass." Both are in love with Brett, and both follow her around blindly and cater to her whims. Cohn, according to Mike, is an "emasculated steer"; Jake is physically emasculated. Although Jake likes to think of himself as a realist, he has elements of the romantic about him, and Cohn would be more realistic if he could. Jake's saving grace, perhaps, is the fact that he can see how much, in truth, he and Cohn resemble each other.

By now Brett cares nothing about either Cohn or Jake—she's in love with Romero. Does she know how to act responsibly? "I've never been able to help anything," she says, admitting that she has no self-control.

NOTE: Remember that Robert Cohn is criticized for having no self-control. By now we understand that none of his so-called friends has self-control, either. But only Cohn—because he's outside the clique, because he's a Jew—is criticized for it.

Brett wants to seduce Romero, and asks Jake to help her get him. As readers, we look down at this spiritual wasteland and see Brett traveling both with her fiancé, Mike, and with her ex-lover, Robert Cohn. And we see her asking Jake, the man she really loves

but can't sleep with, to help her get another man,
Pedro Romero. And Jake does help her. Romero is
rather certain that this English noblewoman is interested in him, but he won't return her interest until
he's absolutely sure. He looks at Jake, and Jake nods
approvingly. It's a humiliating moment for him, and
he's ashamed.

This very important chapter ends with Brett and
Romero going off together. Jake is condemned by the
men who honored him for possessing the rare quality
of *afición*. Mike and Robert Cohn, both of whom feel
they "own" Brett, will soon discover what has happened to her. We can assume that when they find out
that Jake has betrayed them they will give vent to all
their pent-up hostility.

CHAPTER XVII

This is the first of two climactic chapters.

Brett is off with Romero. Jake, Bill, Mike, and Bill's
pick-up, Edna, bluster drunkenly until Cohn shows
up. Where's Brett? he wants to know. Jake lies and
says he doesn't know. Finally Mike tells him she's
with Romero.

Cohn calls Jake a pimp for "selling" Brett to
Romero. Jake throws a punch; Cohn easily ducks. The
fight that's been building between these two grownup schoolboys erupts but ends almost as quickly as it
began. All Cohn has to do is hit Jake once, and Jake
falls down; Cohn hits him again, and the fight is over.
Cohn easily knocks Mike down, too, and then
departs. When their code of manliness is finally put to
the test, everybody fails.

NOTE: That the characters fail, that they fall far
short of their self-imposed code, is what makes the
book complex and not a simple adventure story with

essentially two-dimensional characters. The novel, in fact, can be read as a modern tragedy in which good people are destroyed by fate (the war) and by tragic flaws (personal shortcomings). Each character responds to the postwar world in his own way; whether each is a victim of circumstance or is personally responsible for his fate is something you have to decide for yourself.

Jake is physically shaken. Having acted despicably and then been beaten up by a man he despises, he has obviously lost a good deal of self-esteem. Pay close attention to the paragraph in which he trudges across the plaza, for it is a turning point in the book.

Everything looks "new and changed" to him. "It was all different," he says. If you can remember a time when you received bad news and suddenly felt that you were in a new world, you know how Jake feels. He remembers, as a boy, coming home from an out-of-town football game where he had been kicked in the head, and he remembers dragging a suitcase home from the game, a symbol of his humiliation. Now he's dragging a "phantom suitcase." Now, as then, his whole idea of himself has changed.

Jake tells us he needs a "deep, hot bath, to lie back in." This should remind you of Brett's obsession with bathing as a way of washing away her guilt, and restoring the purity she has lost.

Cohn, meanwhile, is crying, wracked with guilt. He keeps apologizing to Jake, begging Jake to forgive him, and finally Jake relents.

NOTE: Robert Cohn has been enduring a terrible rite of passage, as one by one his romantic illusions are stripped from him. "I just couldn't stand it about Brett," he explains. "I've been through hell, Jake. . . .

When I met her down here Brett treated me as though I were a perfect stranger."

Cohn, the idealist, believed that Brett shared his ideas of romance. As the reader you've known all along how blind he was, but Cohn is only now beginning to understand. The truth is a rude awakening for him, as it would be for anyone whose dreams have been shattered. Before he can pick up the pieces he goes from believing everything to believing nothing. "I guess it isn't any use," he says. "What?" Jake asks. "Everything," Cohn replies.

At this moment Cohn gives up his illusions. He has nothing to believe in now; he has finally become one of the wastelanders. And yet has he? One has the suspicion that he'll never fit into this postwar world, but will go on either believing in the impossible, or lamenting its loss.

Jake finally finds a bathtub, but when he turns on the tap there's no water. Symbolically, the comfort he needs is not to be found. This is the low point for Jake; he can escape only into an exhausted sleep.

When he wakes up he has a headache, but still hurries to the bullring. It's the last day of the fiesta. The bulls are being run through the streets again, chasing the fleeing crowds. A bull catches a man in the back and lifts him into the air, goring him mercilessly.

NOTE: Men are helpless before the bulls, just as the characters in the novel are helpless before the brute force of the world. The man, whose name was Vicente Girones, tempted fate and lost. He had no experience with bulls, unlike Pedro Romero, who had the grace and skill to play with death and survive.

What was the point of Girones' death? Was his heroism cheap and meaningless in the same way the heroism of the soldiers who won medals for their bravery was meaningless to Mike? True glory has left the world, to be replaced by brutal games. "All for fun," the waiter says, implying that this waiter, who lacks *afición*, sees bullfighting as pointless and foolish.

An important question raised by *The Sun Also Rises* is whether bullfighting represents a true and worthwhile test of one's manhood or whether it is just an empty ritual. The waiter thinks it's stupid, but in terms of the book he voices a dissenting opinion. Both Jake, who has *afición*, and Hemingway, who loved bullfights and wrote a book about them called *Death in the Afternoon*, believed, at least superficially, that bullfighting had value. For in risking death, men seem to find some meaning in a fallen world. As you've seen, bullfighting is a true test for Pedro Romero—it proves him a hero. Perhaps Hemingway is saying that if you view bullfighting (or the world itself) with *afición*, it can be beautiful and valuable. But if you lack *afición*, like the waiter or Brett, then bullfighting (or life itself) is just an entertaining but worthless game.

Meaningless or not, Girones' death does win him a moment of glory as his coffin is drawn through the streets to the train that will take it back to his village. That same day Pedro Romero fights the bull that killed Girones. Because it was a good fight, the crowd tells him to cut off the bull's ear. He does so, and gives it to his new love, Brett. But what does Brett do with it? She leaves it "shoved far back in the drawer of the bed-table that stood beside her bed in the Hotel Montoya, in Pamplona." Brett's interest in bullfighting extends only as far as Romero; the rest is a meaningless, even worthless ritual.

Bill and Mike return to Jake's room at the hotel and tell him what he missed when the bulls entered the stadium. How long did it take the steers to quiet the bulls? Bill says one hour; Mike says fifteen minutes.

NOTE: Time, it seems, is relative to how we experience it; it is difficult to judge time accurately in any exciting situation, in the bullring as in the war. What's important here is that bullfighting and the war are seen as similar experiences: both silly and tragic in their way, yet both offering an opportunity for action and heroism otherwise lacking in the modern world.

From Mike we learn what happened to Cohn the night before, after his fight. Cohn had charged off to Romero's room, found Brett there with him, and beat him up badly. In yet another romantic gesture, Cohn tried to take Brett away and "make an honest woman of her." He then felt guilty and tried to shake Romero's hand, just as he succeeded in shaking Jake's hand after beating him up. Romero, however, refused to give in.

NOTE: Here we see a striking difference between Jake and Romero. Jake, perhaps because he doesn't feel very deeply, or because he has no beliefs, is quick to put differences behind him. Romero, the true hero, keeps fighting. Even when his face is bloody, Romero tells Cohn that he'll kill him if he doesn't leave town. Like a hero in an old-time western movie, Romero never gives up. Cohn, who really wants only to be loved, tries to make up and again Romero slugs him. "That's quite a kid," Bill says. To the end, Romero acts the hero.

It's easy to criticize Brett's behavior, but when we learn about her past we have to sympathize with her, too. Ashley, her husband, wouldn't sleep on a bed, only the floor. He threatened to kill her, and each night she had to empty the shells from his gun before going to sleep. "She hasn't had an absolutely happy life," Mike says.

Brett once had illusions about romance and a meaningful love—remember the story about her true love during the war—but her dreams died in the face of reality. Although psychologically wounded, she struggled, like Jake, to improve herself. The two of them should be contrasted to Mike and Bill, who don't try to live serious lives at all.

CHAPTER XVIII

The eating and drinking continue on the last day of the fiesta—the day of the most important bullfight. When Brett appears she is again the goddess of the festival. Jake describes her "walking, her head up, as though the fiesta were being staged in her honor, and she found it pleasant and amusing." She has made love to the hero of the festival, Pedro Romero, and still has everyone else in love with her.

Cohn has hurt Romero seriously, but Romero is going to fight the bulls anyway.

Mike, as usual, looks on, impotent and jealous, though now his feelings are directed toward "a bullfighter," not "a Jew named Cohn." He continues to take his frustrations out on Cohn, however, taunting him like a schoolboy.

Brett is radiantly happy. "I feel altogether changed," she says. Robert Cohn is gone, and she can play the goddess. She also has Romero, the man she loves. Her feelings toward him are not just physical. She has been nursing him since Cohn's attack the night before, and awakening in her self some of the maternal feelings she felt as a volunteer nurse helping a young soldier. (That was the only time, remember, when she ever felt true love.) As a nurse, she discards the cigarette-smoking, mannish role that she usually plays, and finds a degree of fulfillment and happiness. As you'll see, her happiness doesn't last.

Jake and Brett take a walk and wander into a church. The last time they entered a church Brett wasn't admitted because she didn't have a hat. Now no one bars her entrance.

But the experience doesn't work for her. "Let's get out of here," she says. "Makes me damn nervous." Going to church "never does me any good." Although nursing Romero has made her feel as if she were starting a new life, she has fallen too far away from the church's beliefs to start anew with them.

Jake digs up Mike and finds him "on the bed looking like a death mask of himself." Some readers think of Hemingway's characters as living a "death-in-life"; that is, they're alive, but dead in most of the ways we consider human—they can't love, make commitments, or take life seriously. Certainly Mike, a drunk who is loud and abusive even with friends, is a kind of moral zombie, and here he even looks like one. Jake tucks him into bed and heads down to dinner.

Then they go to the last bullfight of the festival.

The three bullfighters, Romero, Marcial, and Belmonte, lead a colorful procession into the ring. The picadors wear gaily colored suits full of spangles. Romero has a gold cape and a three-cornered black hat. A band is playing; the crowd stands and cheers.

Romero takes off his cape and gives it to Brett as a symbol of their love. When she receives it, Jake tells her to spread it out on the railing before her so all can see it, but the sword-handler tells her to keep it folded on her lap. Why? Because Romero wants Brett to know he's thinking of her, but he doesn't want to advertise their love before the crowds.

NOTE: Belmonte, the first matador of the afternoon, was once a very great bullfighter. When one fights a bull, there are two zones, one around the man and another around the bull. If a man stays within his own zone (Hemingway calls it his "terrain") he will be relatively safe, but when he passes into the area close to the bull—where his horns will be, where he can gore you—then the man puts himself in danger. (Don't we all make the same choice, standing safely back from life or grappling with it, risking failure?) Belmonte became famous 15 years ago for moving close to the bull and risking his life every time he fought. When he retired, a legend grew up that he was the bravest bullfighter of all times. When Belmonte was coaxed back from retirement, his fans didn't like him anymore. Belmonte in the flesh could never be as grand as his legend. Also, he chose smaller, safer bulls.

Now the fans love Romero. He is consistently great, always choosing dangerous bulls and fighting them on their "terrain." When they are worthy opponents, he loves and respects them. This afternoon he is fighting for Brett, but not showing off for her, because he's also fighting to please himself. When a person wants to impress another, he sometimes forgets his dignity and does something foolish. Romero never loses his dignity. He is a perfect bullfighter, not a brilliant one. Brilliance can blind you; perfection makes you see more clearly.

Since the first bull is color-blind, Romero must attract him not with his scarlet cape but with his body. Most of the crowd is disappointed by the way Romero steps toward the bull and then retreats. Only a true *aficionado* like Jake can understand the perfection of Romero's performance.

When Romero goes to kill the bull, he rises on his toes, blinds the bull with his cape, and thrusts the sword deeply into him. For a moment Romero and the bull are as one. Romero's next bull, the one who killed Vicente Girones, is big, with good horns and a lively spirit. Romero now looks good to everyone, even those who know nothing about bullfighting. The crowd cheers Romero to keep the fight going. He performs flawlessly, with no tricks and no mystifications.

When Romero kills the bull, his older brother is given permission to slice off the bull's ear and present it to Romero as a trophy. Romero gives the ear to Brett. This is enough tribute for Romero, and he would like to decline when the crowd offers to carry him on its shoulders. But he has no choice, and with an embarrassed look is carried off.

Everybody's tired after the fight and the week-long fiesta. Bill and Jake go off for a last drink. Perhaps they're exhausted, perhaps they're uneasy at having to again face the emptiness of their lives. Jake gets more drunk than he can ever remember. Perhaps it's just as well: when he goes to Mike's room he finds out that Brett has run away with Romero. Of the whole crowd only Bill and Mike are left. He misses all the others.

BOOK III

CHAPTER XIX

The fiesta is over, and the last of the group splits up. Bill is going back to Paris, Mike to Saint Jean de Luz (a French beach town), and Jake to San Sebastian (the Spanish town where Robert Cohn and Brett had their affair) for a week's rest. The three share a car to Bayonne, then go to Biarritz, another beach town, for a drink. They gamble for the drinks, and Mike continues to lose. Finally, like the irresponsible child that he is, Mike says he can't pay his debt. Bill offers to pay for him.

Mike gets dropped off, Bill gets put on a train, and Jake is left alone. Deciding to relax, he buys a New York newspaper and sits leisurely in a café to read it. He's "through with fiestas for a while," and happy to be alone. "A bottle of wine [is] good company," he thinks. Notice how carefully he sets out all the details of his simple pleasures. "If you want people to like you you have only to spend a little money," he muses, with perhaps a touch of irony. (Count Mippipopolous would understand this café very well.) Jake knows he can't buy friendship, but after the hurly-burly of Spain he honestly enjoys the simplicity of having everything decided by money.

Back in San Sebastian, Jake's simple life continues. He checks into the hotel, unpacks, showers, lunches, reads, naps, then heads to the beach for a swim. Afterward he strolls around the town and stops to listen to an orchestra.

The next day is another lazy day for Jake. He eats breakfast and reads newspapers in bed, then goes out for another swim. He is relaxing at his hotel when the concierge (the hotel manager) gives him a telegram from Brett: "AM RATHER IN TROUBLE" it says.

Another telegram comes with the same message. Jake feels responsible for her—although he can't make love with her, he loves her—and immediately makes arrangements to meet her in Madrid.

His pleasant vacation has been ruined, and all because of an impossible love. Again he feels most painfully the difficulty of his position with Brett. He has introduced her to Robert Cohn, then set her up with Pedro Romero, but now that she's in trouble he has to go take care of her. He experiences all the hurt and responsibility of love, but none of the joy. He feels sorry for himself, and with good reason.

In Madrid he goes directly to Brett's hotel. She's in bed, in the middle of a messy room, and seems to Jake small and trembling, like a hurt animal.

Brett has been living with Romero in Madrid. At first he was ashamed of her and wanted her to grow her hair—his friends in the café made fun of him because he was with a mannish woman—but he soon accepted her as she was. He then wanted to marry her so she would stay with him forever. But Brett refused, and finally had to tell Romero to leave. Why? "I'm not going to be one of these bitches that ruins children," she tells Jake. She knows she's bound to corrupt a youth as pure and innocent as Romero, and she makes a grand gesture to save him. He is good and she is not, and she knows that she will ruin him. She's not happy about letting him go—perhaps she really does love him—but she sacrifices her desires for Romero's welfare.

What separates Brett and Jake from the other expatriates is their refusal to submit entirely to the selfish morality of the wasteland. If they can't improve life they can at least decide not to make it worse. In this context, Brett's decision to give up Romero is a heroic act. It redeems her. "Deciding not to be a bitch . . . "

she says, is "sort of what we have instead of God." In other words, she has chosen to behave decently in a faithless world. By choosing good over bad, she makes a moral choice. And this moral choice gives her the same satisfaction that God might have given her in another age. In this postwar world Lady Brett has performed a selfless act that, for a moment at least, makes life bearable.

After a huge meal of roast suckling pig, Jake and Brett find a taxi and ride through the streets of Madrid. One last wistful time Brett thinks about how well she and Jake are suited for each other. Though they can't consummate their love, they do understand each other and they do share similar values.

Jake agrees that they could be happy together, yet his final line, "Isn't it pretty to think so?" is full of bitter irony. It reminds us of all the values they should have in their world—love, faith, purpose, commitment—and how, finally, they have none of them.

A STEP BEYOND

Tests and Answers

TESTS

Test 1

1. During his college years Robert Cohn was a _____ champion
   A. boxer   B. swimmer   C. bullfighter

2. Jake Barnes asserts that "Nobody ever lives _____ their life all the way except . . ."
   A. journalists   B. drunkards
   C. bullfighters

3. Even though they love each other, Jake Barnes _____ and Brett Ashley live separately because of
   A. her parents' wishes
   B. a wound he suffered during the war
   C. her drinking problem

4. The action of the novel takes place in France _____ and
   A. Spain   B. England   C. Italy

5. Jake often feels like crying _____
   A. when he's with Brett
   B. when he hears stories about the war
   C. at night

6. Brett is engaged to be married to _____
   A. Mike Campbell   B. Robert Cohn
   C. Bill Gorton

7. The friend to whom Jake feels closest is _____
   A. Mike Campbell   B. Robert Cohn
   C. Bill Gorton

8. Frances wants   _____
   A. to have Jake arrested
   B. to marry Robert Cohn
   C. to buy a villa outside of Paris

9. Count Mippipopolous espouses the phi-   _____
   losophy that life
   A. is a series of unrelated and meaningless
      events
   B. is a succession of trials that prepare each of
      us for the next phase of our existence
   C. is made up of many pleasures that are
      meant to be enjoyed

10. When Brett lets Jake know that she is   _____
    "interested" in Pedro Romero, Jake
    A. arranges for her to meet Romero
    B. goes on a drinking binge
    C. warns her against making a grave
       mistake

11. What problems does Jake's wound cause him?

12. What is "wrong" with Robert Cohn, at least from the
    viewpoint of Jake and his friends?

13. What is "right" with Pedro Romero, at least from Jake's
    viewpoint?

14. How has Jake changed by the end of the book? What
    has he learned?

Test 2

1. Montoya owns   _____
   A. a bull   B. a hotel   C. a newspaper

2. Brett takes a trip to San Sebastian with   _____
   A. Jake
   B. Count Mippipopolous
   C. Robert Cohn

3. Throughout the novel Hemingway's style is   _____
   characterized by
   A. detailed descriptions and complicated
      sentence constructions
   B. sparse descriptions and ambiguous
      dialogue
   C. grotesque descriptions and omniscient
      narration

4. Of the following characters, the one who is an   _____
   aficionado of the bullfights is
   A. Count Mippipopolous
   B. Montoya
   C. Brett

5. Jake goes fishing with   _____
   A. Frances
   B. Robert Cohn
   C. Bill Gorton

6. A group of street dancers perform a ritual in   _____
   honor of
   A. Jake Barnes
   B. Brett Ashley
   C. a Spanish flag

7. Cohn has a fit of weeping immediately after   _____
   A. he has beaten up Pedro Romero
   B. he sees a man killed at the bullfights
   C. Brett tells him she never wants to see him
      again

8. The character who is usually in debt is   _____
   A. Mike Campbell
   B. Robert Cohn
   C. Belmonte

9. According to Jake, the "national sport" of   _____
   France is
   A. skiing   B. bicycling   C. drinking

10. The two telegrams that Jake receives from _____
    Brett are essentially
    A. pleas for him to help her
    B. reports of Cohn's unbalanced behavior
    C. promises that she will soon return to him

11. Discuss the Hemingway style.

12. What does love mean to Jake, Brett, and Robert Cohn?

13. What does bullfighting represent in the novel?

14. "Isn't it pretty to think so?" Jake says to Brett's statement that they could have had a very good time together. What does he mean by this?

ANSWERS

Test 1

1. A   2. C   3. B   4. A   5. C   6. A
7. C   8. B   9. C   10. A

11.   His wound makes Jake impotent, incapable of making love. The torture of his wound, though, is that he can still feel desire. For a year now he and Lady Brett Ashley have been in love, but Jake's wound has kept them from consummating it. They're in a seemingly eternal hell of thwarted desire—both desperately want something that they cannot have.

Point out that Jake is defined by this wound. He's always thinking about it, even when he doesn't seem to be. Mention that whenever he's about to go to bed, and his thoughts loosen, he thinks about his wound and Brett.

Jake's wound also reflects the sickness of postwar society. This can be called the Fisher King interpretation, referring to T. S. Eliot's poem "The Waste Land." Jake, like the Fisher King, has become a living symbol of a sterile world in which nothing grows or flourishes. Jake tries both the church and love, but neither works for him. *The Sun Also Rises* is a bleak book because of the apparent inevitability of Jake's impotence.

12. The first strike against Cohn, at least in the eyes of his so-called friends, is that he's a Jew. Whether Hemingway failed to find this anti-Semitism repugnant (he was writing years before Hitler began his program to exterminate the Jews), or whether he used anti-Semitism merely as a window into the minds of his characters is something you'll want to discuss in your answer.

Being a Jew automatically makes Cohn an outsider. He was never accepted at Princeton, and he's not accepted in the Bohemian Left Bank of Paris where, ostensibly, he's among friends. Everybody makes fun of him behind his back.

There are some good reasons to ridicule him, though. For one, Cohn's a hopeless romantic among realists. He's gotten his notions from books, not from life itself. The fantasy that sets the book in motion is that he and Brett are storybook lovers; in truth, she goes off with him because she's bored. Cohn can't shake his fantasy, even when Brett turns on him and her fiancé Mike arrives. Cohn continues to follow Brett around like a puppy, embarrassing her and humiliating himself.

Cohn has another problem: his lack of self-awareness. He can't see when he's making a nuisance of himself. He is self-conscious and full of self-doubt. The other characters think Cohn a fool, in part because they need a scapegoat for their own failings. Making fun of Cohn relieves them of their own frustrations and gives them a sense of power missing in their own lives.

You should also realize that Cohn's romantic obsession has a sort of nobility to it. At least he believes in true love (nobody else does except perhaps Pedro Romero). Cohn is, in a sense, a modern-day equivalent of a chivalric hero. Perhaps, like Don Quixote, his real problem is that he's living in the wrong age.

13. First you might discuss the way Belmonte fights. He is the bullfighter who once was great but who is now a parody of himself. Hemingway contrasts him with Romero. "Romero did always, smoothly, calmly, and beautifully, what he, Belmonte, could only bring himself to do now sometimes."

Now turn to Jake's long description of Romero fighting a bull in Chapter XVIII. Two key sentences say much about him: "It was not brilliant bull-fighting. It was only perfect bull-fighting." In other words, Romero is not a showoff; he performs for the sake of his art, not merely to impress his audience. What he does he does simply, purely, perfectly. No gestures are wasted. He fights partly for Brett (because he loves her) but mostly for himself. He has his own standards and works tirelessly to meet them.

Even after Romero fights beautifully, he remains modest. In his last fight, when the crowd wants to carry him triumphantly on their shoulders, he concedes reluctantly. He has already satisfied himself; to be worshipped by an unruly mob makes him uncomfortable.

Why does Jake like Romero? He is the personification of Jake's ideal of the hero. He stands for what Jake himself would like to be, but can't.

14. You might start to answer this question by asking, What hasn't changed for Jake? His wound is still affecting his whole life. He still loves Brett, and she him, but they cannot consummate their love. He's not any happier, and his life doesn't seem to have changed in any great way. He will return to Paris and continue his life as a journalist.

He has learned some things, however. In his search for meaning he has found Pedro Romero, who embodies the values he seeks. He has also learned that when he's in serious trouble, he can't live up to his values.

Some readers, including Hemingway, see the story as a tragedy, with Jake as the tragic hero. On a personal level *The Sun Also Rises* is the portrait of a single man who has a vision of a better life, aspires to it, and fails to attain it. On a wider, social level (the Fisher King interpretation) Jake is symbolic of a lost generation—all casualties, in some way, of World War I—who, try as they may, cannot make anything grow in a sterile world.

In real terms none of the characters changes, grows happy, or improves. They simply live out their fate, whether it's Brett as Circe, Cohn as a romantic fool, Mike as a drunk, or Jake as an impotent, tormented soul.

Test 2

1. B   2. C   3. B   4. B   5. C   6. B
7. A   8. A   9. B   10. A

11. Hemingway used simple words, preferably nouns and verbs, and arranged them in rhythmic patterns that roll naturally off the tongue. Speak some aloud. He also liked to repeat words and phrases that produced a chantlike, almost hypnotic effect.

Hemingway believed that the best writing results when words simply describe the stimuli that produce an emotion. His secret was to choose his words with great care, using language that most directly represented the object or feeling itself, uncluttered with "tricks and mystifications." Count Mippipopolous says that the secret of making friends is not to "joke" people; that's also one of the secrets of Hemingway's successful style. Honesty was his keynote; he worked tirelessly to rid his prose of sensationalism and sentiment.

Hemingway compared good writing to the tip of an iceberg. He believed that if you know your subject thoroughly, you can achieve the full effect by describing just a small portion of it and implying the rest. You know from writing papers that when you know your subject well a few words can say everything. When a subject is unclear to you, you need to write twice as much to explain yourself, and the parts of your paper still won't hold together. There's no substitute, Hemingway believed, for a thorough knowledge of your entire subject.

12.   Jake can feel love, but he can't express it or consummate it. Because of his wound, physical desire is a torture to him. His feelings for Brett well up in the middle of the night and are so painful that he can't sleep. (In this modern wasteland, emotions that should bring happiness, such as love, can often be the most painful.)

Brett once loved a young soldier whom she cared for when she was a nurse, but he died and none of her other relationships—with her neurotic husband or with ineffectual lovers—has satisfied her. Robert Cohn calls her Circe, suggesting that she bewitches men and turns them into swine. Brett herself tells Jake not to love her because she'll only deceive him. Love, for Brett, has become a power she wields. It changes men but leaves her unmoved.

For Robert Cohn, love is a storybook romance, like the one he read about in *The Purple Land*, a silly book about an aging Englishman finding love in a romantic country. Cohn has old-fashioned notions of love—he believes in commitment, for instance—but he's too blind to realize that his kind of love is lost among Jake's crowd of friends. Whether his blindness makes him noble or foolish depends on your own definition of love.

13.   Many of the conflicts and themes that occur in the novel are reflected in the bullring and in the language of bullfighting. Mike Campbell, for instance, calls Robert Cohn

a "poor bloody steer." Steers are emasculated bulls used to herd and calm the real bulls before a bullfight. Mike means that Cohn is less than a man. The true steer here, because of his wound, is Jake Barnes. And, of course, the drunken Mike Campbell is anything but manly. Pedro Romero is the only one of the characters capable of fighting the bulls (both in reality and symbolically).

The bullfight is also a "moment of truth" where a man's true worth is demonstrated in a life-or-death situation. Some stand back from the bull as they stand back from life; others enter the bull's zone and are rewarded with victory or death. The struggle between Jake and Cohn for Brett can be read as a bullfight, with Mike as the picador goading them both on. This struggle leads to their moment of truth, when both Jake and Cohn have to accept their ultimate failure.

14. Jake is being bitterly ironic here. If nothing else, you have seen that no love will ever work out between Jake and Brett, as much as they, in moments of weakness, wish it would. And yet they can't stop hoping. In a way it is Brett's final wistful hope that is their saving grace.

Jake's ironic phrase is also perfectly hardboiled—it recognizes how the world should be a place where love, faith, God, and *afición* triumph, yet how, in their world, none of these things does succeed. Throughout the book Jake has been trying to look over a wall to what is possible, always seeing the better world on the other side. His perception of a better world is what sets him apart from the other characters, who settle within their wasteland world.

It's "pretty to think" that there is a better world, that they will find fulfillment in love, but all they have is a "pretty picture" of what will never be. Better wistful hope, however, than the utter helplessness of someone like Mike.

Term Paper Ideas

1. Discuss Robert Cohn's relations with women: his first wife, Frances, and Lady Brett Ashley.

2. How does Jake Barnes feel about Robert Cohn? Why does he feel this way?

3. Why is Robert Cohn's reading of *The Purple Land* sinister, as Jake claims it is?

4. At the *bal musette*, Jake makes fun of Braddocks, Frances, and others. What does he find wrong with them? Is he fair?

5. Why does Jake say, in the *bal musette*, "The whole show makes me sick"? What would he like better?

6. Jake's given name, Jacob, is "a hell of a Biblical name," according to Brett. Who is Jacob in the Bible, and why would Jake Barnes be named after him?

7. What makes Cohn such a romantic? Where does it get him?

8. Why are Jake, Brett, and Count Mippipopolous such realists?

9. Jake says, "It's a lot of fun to be in love." Brett says, "I think it's hell on earth." Discuss their love and why it is doomed to fail.

10. Discuss Count Mippipopolous' system of values. Do Jake and Brett agree with it? Do you?

11. Why does Brett go to San Sebastian with Robert Cohn?

12. What happens to Jake and Bill in the Spanish countryside? What is it about the land that changes them so?

13. What are the differences between the tourists on the train and the Spanish peasants on the bus?

14. Discuss the way Hemingway paints the Spanish countryside so beautifully with words.

15. Why is Jake a "rotten Catholic"?

16. Why does "one lose track of days up here in the mountains"? Compare Paris, Burguete, and Pamplona.

17. Mike calls Cohn a steer. Discuss Hemingway's characters in terms of steers and bulls.

18. Why does Cohn call Brett "Circe"?

19. Why is Jake afraid of the dark? What does he think about when he's alone at night?

20. Why do the Spaniards want Brett "as an image to dance around" during the fiesta?

21. Why does Brett like Romero so much?

22. Why does Mike constantly taunt Cohn, especially for being Jewish?

23. Why does Montoya get silently angry at Jake and finally refuse to talk to him?

24. Why is Jake carrying a "phantom suitcase" after Cohn knocks him out?

25. Why does Cohn apologize so profusely to Jake after hitting him?

28. "Bulls are brute animals," says a waiter after Vicente Girones is gored. Discuss why he believes bullfights are stupid.

29. Why does Jake think bullfights are grand? What is the nature of his *afición*?

30. Why is the bullfighter Belmonte jeered by the crowd? Why is Romero cheered?

31. Why does Brett call Jake to Madrid?

32. What is it that Brett "sort of [has] instead of God"?

Further Reading

CRITICAL WORKS

Baker, Carlos. *Ernest Hemingway: A Life Story*. New York: Scribner's, 1969.

_____. *Hemingway: The Writer as Artist*, 3rd ed. Princeton: Princeton University Press, 1964.

_____, ed. *Hemingway and His Critics: An International Anthology*. New York: Hill & Wang, 1961.

_____. *Ernest Hemingway: Critiques of Four Major Novels*. New York: Scribner's, 1962.

Baker, Sheridan. *Ernest Hemingway: An Introduction and Interpretation*. New York: Holt, Rinehart and Winston, 1967.

Donaldson, Scott. *By Force of Will: The Life and Art of Ernest Hemingway*. New York: Viking, 1977.

Fenton, Charles A. *The Apprenticeship of Ernest Hemingway: The Early Years*. New York: Farrar, Straus & Cudahy, 1954.

Grebstein, Sheldon Norman. *Hemingway's Craft*. Carbondale: Southern Illinois University Press, 1973.

Hemingway, Ernest. "The Unpublished Opening of The Sun Also Rises." *Antaeus*, Spring 1979, pp. 7–14.

Killinger, John. *Hemingway and the Dead Gods*. University of Kentucky, 1960.

Lee, A. Robert, ed. *Ernest Hemingway: New Critical Essays*. Totowa, N.J.: Barnes and Noble, 1983.

Lewis, Robert W., Jr. *Hemingway on Love*. Austin: University of Texas Press, 1965.

Plimpton, George, ed. *Writers at Work: The Paris Review Interviews*. New York: Viking, 1963.

Rovit, Earl. *Ernest Hemingway*. New York: Twayne, 1963.

Sarason, Bertram D., ed. *Hemingway and the Sun Set*. Washington, D.C.: NCR, 1972.

Shaw, Samuel. *Ernest Hemingway*. New York: Frederick Ungar, 1973.

Weeks, Robert P., ed. *Hemingway: A Collection of Critical Essays.* Englewood Cliffs, N.J.: Prentice-Hall, 1962.

White, William, ed. *Studies in "The Sun Also Rises."* Columbus, Ohio: Charles E. Merrill, 1969.

Williams, Wirt. *The Tragic Art of Ernest Hemingway.* Baton Rouge: Louisiana State University Press, 1981.

Young, Philip. *Ernest Hemingway.* New York, 1952.

AUTHOR'S OTHER WORKS

In Our Time (1924)

The Torrents of Spring (1926)

Men Without Women (1927)

A Farewell to Arms (1929)

Death in the Afternoon (1932)

Winner Take Nothing (1933)

Green Hills of Africa (1935)

To Have and Have Not (1937)

First Forty-Nine Stories (1938)

For Whom the Bell Tolls (1940)

Across the River and Into the Trees (1950)

The Old Man and the Sea (1952)

A Moveable Feast (posthumous, 1964)

Islands in the Stream (posthumous, 1970)

The Nick Adams Stories (posthumous, 1972)

Glossary

Note: entries dealing with bullfighting are marked with an asterisk and are Hemingway's own definitions from his book about bullfighting, *Death in the Afternoon*.

Absinthe A green, bitter liqueur with the flavor of wormwood and anise.

Afición (Sp.) Passion, as Jake Barnes explains it; a devotion so complete as to make one more than an expert.

Angel Someone who supports the arts financially, who hovers around the arts, keeping them alive.

Arriba (Sp.) Get on up!

Arriero (Sp.) A man who drives mules; muleteer.

Bal musette (Fr.) Low-class dance hall.

***Barrera** (Sp.) The red painted wooden fence around the sanded ring in which the bull is fought. The first row of seats are also called barreras.

Bateau mouche (Fr.) Pleasure boat on the Seine River in Paris.

Bayonne French town near the Spanish border.

Biarritz French resort on the Atlantic, near the Spanish border.

Brioche (Fr.) Breakfast roll.

Burguete Spanish hill town near where Jake and Bill go fishing.

Centime Unit of French currency, one hundredth of a franc, similar to an American penny.

Che Mala Fortuna! (It.) What bad luck!

Circe The enchantress who in Homer's *Odyssey* bewitched men and turned them into swine.

Cogido (Sp.) Seized; picked up and gored by a bull.

Col A gap between mountain ranges, used as a pass.

Concierge (Fr.) Doorkeeper or superintendent of an apartment building; the manager of a hotel.

*Cornada (Sp.) A horn wound; a real wound as distinct from a bruising scratch.

Darb (slang) A person or thing considered excellent (Bill uses it ironically in reference to Cohn).

Diligence A public stagecoach used in France.

*Encierro (Sp.) The driving of fighting bulls on foot, surrounded by steers, from one corral to the corral of the ring. In Pamplona this refers to the running of the bulls through the streets with the crowd running ahead of them.

Fine (Fr.) Ordinary brandy.

Flamenco (Sp.) A very lively Andalusian gypsy song and dance, with snapping castanets and clicking heels.

Gentille (Fr.) Pleasant and kind.

Globos illuminados (Sp.) Paper sacks set on fire that fly up like flaming balloons; part of the festival at Pamplona.

Hardboiled Slang for a tough guy whom nothing affects.

Irati River River in Spain's Basque province where Bill and Jake go fishing.

Jota (Sp.) Spanish folk dance and music.

Lourdes A town in southwest France with a famous Roman Catholic shrine. Millions of pilgrims go there yearly.

*Matador (Sp.) A killer of bulls in a bullfight.

Mattock A tool for loosening the soil; like a pickaxe, but with a flat blade.

Mencken, H. L. American editor and columnist known for his iconoclastic view of middle-class America; a model for young people in the 1920s.

*Muleta (Sp.) Heart-shaped scarlet cloth of serge or flannel, folded and doubled over a tapered wooden stick equipped with a sharp steel point at the narrow end and a grooved handle at the widened extremity. The muleta is used to defend the bullfighter; to tire the bull and regulate the position of his head and feet; to perform a series of passes of more or less aesthetic value with the bull; and to aid the bullfighter in the killing.

Ney's Statue . A statue of Marshal Ney in Paris. Ney was one of the most celebrated of Napoleon's generals.

Ospedale Maggiore Hospital in Milan, Italy, where Jake recuperated after being wounded in the war.

Pamplona Mountain town in the Basque provinces of Spain where the annual festival of San Fermín is held.

Patronne (Fr.) Manager (here of a nightclub).

Pelota (Sp.) A Spanish game like handball.

Pesetas (Sp.) Spanish money.

*Picador (Sp.) A man who pics bulls from on horseback under the orders of a matador.

Pimp Slang term for a man who sets other men up with prostitutes.

Poule (Fr.) Slang for chick, girl.

*Quite (Sp.) The taking away of the bull from anyone who has been placed in immediate danger by him. It especially refers to the taking away of the bull from the horse and man after he has charged the picadors.

Riau-riau Wild music played during the festival of San Fermín.

Saint Jean de Luz Small French resort town near the Spanish border, where Mike Campbell goes after the fiesta.

San Sebastian Beautiful old Spanish town near the French border on the Bay of Biscay.

Sommelier (Fr.) Wine steward.

V.A.D. Voluntary Aid Detachment, a group of volunteer nurses during World War I. Brett was one of them.

*Veronica (Sp.) Pass with the cape as the bull charges.

Wickets Turnstiles going into the bullfighting arena.

The Critics

This is a novel about a lady. Her name is Lady Ashley and when the story begins she is living in Paris and it is Spring. That should be a good setting for a romantic but highly moral story. . . .

So my name is Jacob Barnes and I am writing the story, not as I believe is usual in these cases, from a desire for confession, because being a Roman Catholic I am spared that Protestant urge to literary production, nor to set things all out the way they happened for the good of some future generation, nor for any other of the usual highly moral urges, but because I believe it is a good story. . . .

Cohn is the hero.

> —*Ernest Hemingway, from the original opening chapters to* The Sun Also Rises, *deleted before publication of the novel*

But to say that the sun *also* rises is to emphasize that it has set. The sun also rises, yes, and the earth abides, yes; but our generation is no longer here to rise nor to stay; and the ancient classical sadness of this fact echoes Biblically and beautifully underneath everything in Barnes's meditation on the past, underneath the bright moments. . . .

Jake Barnes represents the best of the lost generation, the best that is lost.

> —*Sheridan Baker*, Ernest Hemingway, 1967

Hemingway has written the courtly romance for moderns, tough, dissonant, yet echoing forever the ancient sweetness of being forever lovelorn and forever longing, all underlined by the final knowledge of damnation, knowing that it never could have been, yet doomed to think that it might.

> —*Sheridan Baker*, Ernest Hemingway, 1967

Without the war as a causative background these would be merely empty and sick people who drain their lives away into the receding blue notes of a jazz orchestra; but the war was a fact, and it was one which stripped the veil of pious sanctimony and patriotic veneer from the spurious moralities and ethics or traditional American "boosterism" in religion, philosophy, and politics.

—*Earl Rovit*, Ernest Hemingway, *1963*

One of the most persistent themes of the twenties was the death of love in World War I. All the major writers recorded it. . . .

This fear of emotional consequences is the key to Barnes's condition. Like so many Hemingway heroes, he has no way to handle subjective complications, and his wound is a token of his impotence. . . . Whoever bears his sickness well is akin to Barnes; whoever adopts false postures, or willfully hurts others, falls short of his example. . . .

Like the many victims of romantic literature, from Don Quixote to Tom Sawyer, [Cohn] lives by what he reads and neglects reality at his own and others' peril.

—*Mark Spilka, in* Studies in
The Sun Also Rises, *1969*

And yet *The Sun Also Rises* is still Hemingway's *Waste Land*, and Jake is Hemingway's *Fisher King*. This may just be coincidence, though the novelist had read the poem, but once again here is the protagonist gone impotent, and his land gone sterile. Eliot's London is Hemingway's Paris, where spiritual life in general, and Jake's sexual life in particular, are alike impoverished. Prayer breaks down, . . . a knowledge of traditional distinctions between good and evil is largely lost, copulation is morally neutral and, cut off from the past chiefly by the spiritual disaster of the war, life has become mostly meaningless. "What shall we do?" is the same constant question, to which the answer must be, again, "Nothing."

—*Philip Young*, Ernest Hemingway,
1952